'One Day I'll See You'

'One Day I'll See You'

By Peter Jackson

with Helena Rogers

AMBASSADOR

One Day I'll See You
© Copyright 1993 Peter Jackson and Helena Rogers
Ambassador Edition 1993

All Rights Reserved

ISBN 0 907927 90 4

Ambassador Productions Ltd.
PROVIDENCE HOUSE
16 HILLVIEW AVENUE,
BELFAST-BT5 6JR
UNITED KINGDOM

CONTENTS

Acknowledgements

Grateful thanks to:

The Royal National Institute for the Blind

The Guide Dogs for the Blind Association

Mrs. Slater of Sittingbourne,

who enabled me to visualise a 'Taylor Frame'

FOREWORD

By Dave Pope

It is unusual to find people who talk openly about dying!
Therefore, imagine my surprise when, as a teenager, I sat down
for a snack lunch with Peter Jackson, and halfway through my
tuna sandwich he suddenly declared, 'You know Dave, I'm
really looking forward to the day when I die!'
This is not usually the subject of conversation on a Friday lunch
time in the middle of Birmingham so, sensing my surprise, Peter
added, 'Well you see Dave, I've never seen the face of my wife
and children, but the first face I shall see will be that of Jesus.'
I could have kicked myself being so naive!
My association with Peter began in the late '60s when I was
completing my studies in Behavioural Psychology at Aston
University and, as Friday mornings found me ploughing my
way through lectures and tutorials on statistical analysis, I was
normally delighted to take time out for lunch in the centre of
Birmingham. I would sometimes visit a large department store,
and visit to top floor which housed the Art and Music Department, and one day as the escalator transported me to that floor,
I heard the strains of music that I recognised. Gospel music in
Rackhams on Friday afternoon? - a little unusual to say the least!
But it all became clear as I discovered a piano tuner assessing the
quality of his workmanship by playing his own special brand of
music - and gathering an audience, and customers for the store
at the same time. I soon developed a friendship with this piano
tuner and his wife Margaret, and discovered a source of tremen-

dous encouragement, as well as a wealth of talent. Peter Jackson - the blind pianist - already established as a well loved and well respected minister soon became my mentor as I enjoyed being a 'Timothy'. Subsequently, Peter and I spent many hours together; I drove him to Evangelistic meetings, and used the opportunity to soak up all the advice that I could receive from someone so 'in tune' with the Lord.

In the years that followed, God led both of us into wider ministry opportunity. This book documents Peter's story; fascinating to say the least, and one that I hope will encourage many more to take risks in order to accomplish what is on God's heart.

Chapter 1

SOUNDS OF LONELINESS

The shock, when it came, was essentially my mothers. The consultant looked gravely across his imposing desk and stated flatly:

"I'm afraid this child will be blind for life."

At the age of sixteen months, I had been taken into hospital for surgery on what was described as a 'tubercular gland' in my neck. The operation was performed, but an epidemic of measles broke out in the hospital, and in my weakened state I could not avoid it. The infection attacked my optic nerves causing inflammation and swelling, and the specialist confirmed that they had atrophied. My eyes would have to be removed.

My mother was at her wit's end. She was not only horrified at the tragedy of the situation, but she had four children under seven years of age, and was four months pregnant with her next baby. How could she possibly manage the colossal problem of a blind toddler?

To begin with there was never enough money. In 1933, my father's job was an interesting one - he was a gold beater making gold leaf for books and other specialist items - but it did not provide a wage which was sufficient to support a large family and a fairly frequent glass of beer. My mother was obliged to work in order to help feed the family, and she somehow managed to look after babies at the same time. This new calamity, however, was too much to bear. It was not only a disaster for me, but for my whole family.

The authorities advised her.

"There is a solution, Mrs.Jackson," my distraught mother was told. "The National Institute for the Blind has a home for blind babies at Leamington Spa. When Peter is two years old in a few months' time, he could leave home and go to live there. In this way he would receive the expert help which he needs to enable him to cope adequately in a sighted world."

It was not an easy decision for my mother. On the one hand she would be abandoning her little boy into the hands of strangers, but on the other, she had no idea how to teach me, let alone earn a living and look after the rest of the family at the same time! She really had no choice, and with a heavy heart she agreed.

My admission to the 'Sunshine Homes' and institutional living with the benefit of those who could teach me what I needed to know, did not impress me at the age of two. Being catapulted into blindness left me desperate for familiar sounds. I wanted to hear the voices of my brother and two sisters; the noise of my mother preparing food in the kitchen; the sound of horses' hooves and traffic on the Birmingham streets, and even my father's irritable shouts.

Instead, everything changed. I was taken to a strange place with unfamiliar sounds and new smells; there were unknown voices and different echoes in the rooms. Nothing was the same, and I was desolate. Now and again my mother came to visit me, but I detected a change in our relationship which filled me with uneasiness as I clung to her. All I wanted was to be taken home to all the old sounds and familiarity. But she did not come to take me home, and although she hugged me and my eager fingers felt the tears on her face, I fearfully knew she would leave me again.

I could not calculate the time between her visits - they were simply unexpected surprises. But the surprises became even less often when the authorities decreed that the home at Leamington Spa should have a change of purpose. Much later I found out that it became a home for retarded blind babies, while the 'normal' ones would move to a new home a long way away in East Grinstead, Sussex.

The new 'Sunshine Home' was a rehabilitation centre where my training began in earnest.

As time went by, the staff here took the place of my family, and the other children that of my brothers and sisters. I remembered my old home and family, but they gradually became more and more distant, as the sounds and feel of the East Grinstead home became more familiar to me.

There was rigid routine. We got up and went to bed at the same times, we ate together at the same time and always in the same place. We played in the same room with the same toys, and walked or played outside on the same grass.

There were notable consistencies: for instance, when we woke in the morning, there would be a Rich Tea biscuit lying beside our heads on the pillow - not a digestive or a shortbread - a Rich Tea - always a Rich Tea. It was unfailingly there, and we knew when we awoke that we could stretch out a hand and touch it.

When we were dressed we would go to breakfast in the dining room. We were taught how to carry a tray so that what was on it did not slide off, and we learned how to eat properly, using (at this early age) just a spoon; and we were shown how to hold a cup.

The consistencies of eating were impressed upon us:

"No, Peter. You must hold your bread in your other hand - your *left* hand," my teacher insisted, 'and your drinking glass always stands on the *right*." She gripped the appropriate hand as she spoke.

Most of our day was spent in the playroom where there was a see-saw and a rocking horse, and things that rattled or made a noise. A musical box fascinated me. Its tinkling sound and changing notes seemed to demand my attention and I sat, enthralled, to listen to it. There was also a bird cage which held a toy canary. When it was wound up, it would trill a brilliant song. Other toys did not mean much. They were just shapes to be felt, but as there was not much difference to their feel, we were happier with moving or noisy toys.

Outside we could play on the grass and smell the trees. I loved the smell of the wood, and liked to feel the rough texture of the bark and breathe in its scent. There was one tree, however, which smelled better than any others - and this one was not outside, but actually indoors!

At Christmas time a tree was put up in the playroom. What excitement there was on the day when the door was opened and we went into the room to be met by that pungent smell! It seemed to embody happiness, excitement, fun and an indefinable togetherness, for this was the time when Father Christmas would come to visit us.

We were all taught to believe strongly in Father Christmas. Hardly any of us knew our real fathers, and if we had ever known one, they were by this time dim and misty figures.

Women were the dominant factors in our lives, and men hardly figured at all. So Father Christmas was a loving father of the kind none of us had known. He visited us rarely, of course, but when he came he always brought a present, and we looked forward to his coming with a mixture of awe, fascination and love. As each year passed by, Christmas took on an increasing significance which could shatter our happiness if anything occurred to alter our expectations.

The days and months passed by slowly and monotonously, until the summer returned once again. But this time of year brought a different kind of treat - a day at the seaside.

It was not only the new surroundings with its irresistible sounds and smells that made us almost delirious with delight. It began from the moment we left the home, because the journey was always made in cars.

Like all little boys, I loved cars. I liked to hear the noise of the engine, and the way it changed pitch as it got up speed; I loved the seats with their leathery smell and interesting cracks and shiny patches; and then there was the smell of the petrol which became synonymous with anticipation and excitement. We squashed together on the back seat, savouring every moment. The seaside was full of scents and sounds. The fishy smell of the ozone; the sound of the breeze as it flapped at the windbreaks and sometimes took our breath away; the variety of noises on the beach - children laughing and shouting and maybe the 'thwack' of a ball hit by a bat or caught in the hand. Even the ever present coming and going of traffic on the nearby road somehow seemed gloriously different from the sound of the traffic at home.

But best of all , we loved to listen to the sound we could not hear anywhere else - the noise of the sea. Sometimes the waves were small and we could paddle about with the water splashing to our knees, but sometimes the waves crashed onto the sand so that it felt as though we might be pushed over if an unexpectedly big wave came. This was part of the excitement - we could listen to the sand being dragged back into the sea, and hear it hover for a moment or two before crashing to the beach. If we judged the length of the dragging correctly, we could tell how big the wave would be as it fell, and we would race backwards with screams of laughter before we were soaked! But misjudge the sounds - and you could be hit full in the chest and fall over, gasping for breath!

Then when we were tired, we would sit on the sand and make sand pies. How we loved the feel of the sand. On one part of the beach it would be warm and dry, and we could run the smooth grains from one hand to the other; but nearer the sea it was damp and we could make rows of sand pies which we could smash down with out feet, screaming with delight at the same time!

Even the rain could not dampen our spirits on one of these rare days out. So long as we could be kept dry, it was nice to listen to the raindrops pattering on the road, or even more loudly on an umbrella over our heads.But if there should be a storm with thunder.......! How I loved the thunder! The distant rumbling that built up sometimes slowly to recede disappointingly to nothing only to begin again a few minutes later; but sometimes it went on and on more urgently until it gave way to a rolling crash which made me gasp with wonder! It was a glorious, awesome noise and I clapped my hands joyfully every time!

One day, when I was four years old, we had an outing which was unique, and must have been one of those times when the staff were more nervous than us! We were invited to the Mansion House in London, to have tea with the Lord Mayor. We could not have understood then, but it was to include a presentation to the National Institute for the Blind, and a recognition of their work. (This was before it had its 'Royal' status).

We were on our best behaviour. Excitement was mixed with apprehension as we were threatened with dire punishments if we forgot our manners.

"Sit still!" said our teachers. "Keep quiet, and do as you are told!"

The journey was undertaken with suppressed exhilaration, which gradually gave way to nervousness as the lower, more intense roar of the London traffic met our ears. By the time we reached our destination, we were struck dumb with the enormousness of the occasion, and our good behaviour was assured.

We climbed the steps of the Mansion House, conscious of the many people rushing past us who all seemed to be going to important appointments like us; and were then ushered into the hall where we were to have tea. I could tell that there were a lot of people present, all talking excitedly, but their voices had an echoing quality which my young ears were unable to interpret. I had never been in a room so large, so I could not fully understand the vastness of the place until I put the memories into context as I grew up.

Even the food was different. As this was tea, I could confidently and delicately explore the contents of my plate as I had been taught. This was not the bread and jam which we were used to. It was certainly bread - I could tell that by its texture of course, but the sandwich was neatly cut into an unusual shape. Much later I was able to define it as having been a triangle, but at the time I was overcome by the novelty of such a thing! It was all very wonderful and completely overwhelming!

On the return journey home, most of us were overtaken by tiredness and sleep, but there cannot have been one child who would forget the wonder of the day which we spent at The Mansion House with The Lord Mayor.

Back in our usual routine I had to be content with more mundane pleasures, although there was always one thing that attracted my attention. In the corridor which led down to the playroom, an extension speaker had been fixed through which we could hear the radio. In those days it was called the 'wireless', but it was a source of delight to us all. Many wonderful sounds came from it, but some stirred my imagination more than others.

In the first place, it was the gong which was used to call us in at mealtimes which attracted my attention. It was not an indefinable clanging, but a device which gave out several different notes. I listened to it carefully, noting the changes in pitch. The wireless however, was a different matter. One sound in particular fascinated me more than any other.

Between programmes there would occasionally be an interlude during which the sound of the Bow Bells was played. This was no simple affair like the dinner gong, but a glorious cacophony of interwoven ringing which held me spellbound until it finally died away and the next programme began. I would shut out the unwelcome new sound, and try to hold onto the beautiful melody of the bells for as long as possible. How I wished that they would play them more often!

The world of a toddler revolves largely around himself. This is particularly true of the blind toddler who is unable to interact with his peers by sight. Add to this the fact that we were too small to talk much to one another and the world becomes a small, rather introverted circle, punctuated by the necessary direction from our teachers. Discipline was seen as necessary to a child's upbringing and was rigorously applied. Occasionally we would fall out with one another, and I did resort once in frustration to smacking one of the other children. The smack was soundly returned by a teacher, and I responded to the injustice by sitting on the floor and screaming for some time!

I got to know very few of the other children, who were all busy in their own worlds. In later years we were more able to form friendships, but at this early stage, we were 'loners" on the whole.

Even the staff were often unmemorable helpers, but sometimes one stood out among the rest. Miss Clark was a beloved teacher whose tender attention to her deprived charges was never forgotten by any of them. Another much loved member of staff was Matron Johnson, who was dedicated to her job, and had a real love for the dependent children in her care. Her gentle touch and caring manner left lasting memories in all our minds.

One day she tried to prepare me for the inevitable. With her hand placed lightly on my head, in a sign of warmth which would be achieved by sighted people in a look, she said gently:

" You're going to leave us soon, Peter."

I did not understand straightaway but responded instinctively with a dismayed look. She continued instantly,

"You're going to the big school."

I began now to feel a real fear. I did not want to move again. This was my home and I had become dependent on the teachers and staff. Surely they would not abandon me - I thought that they loved me. My mother had almost abandoned me, I rarely saw her now and I could not bear to leave my replacement family and begin all over again.

" I don't want to go." I retorted in desperation.

"I'm afraid that you must." replied Matron firmly, but kindly.

My mother was with me when the day came for the dreaded move to the big school. I was glad to have her with me but I was filled with foreboding. I clung to her hand as the goodbyes were said. I was being let down once more by those I loved most.

My mother told me later that Matron had tears in her eyes as she stood at the door to wave goodbye.

At five years old there was to be a whole new hurdle to overcome in my young life.

Chapter 2

A HARSH WORLD

On September the third, 1936, I left East Grinstead with the other children who were ready for 'the big school'. In the company of a teacher we began the long journey to the Birmingham Royal Institute for the Blind at Harborne - or 'the BRIB' as it came to be called.

We did not say much as we went first by car into London, then on the train, and finished the last leg of the journey to the school by taxi. I was past tears. At five years old I was learning that life never seemed to stay happy. Just when you thought it was turning out right, something happened to change it all again.

My heart thumped in fear and I clung to a teacher's hand as we got out of the taxi and stepped onto the gravel drive. Our feet crunched their way reluctantly to the school door and we went in. By now I knew that the resonant sounds of feet and voices meant that the place was very large. I leaned closer to my teacher. There was a strange smell to the corridors which I later came to understand to be a combination of carbolic, floor polish and stale stew! It was not the comfortable smell of my last school. There was so much rush! Urgent footsteps told me that everyone was in a hurry. They pushed by us, or we had to move out of the way to let them pass as we were ushered to the office and introduced to the Matron. Soon I had been formally admitted.

When the formalities were over, my teacher left to return to East Grinstead, and once more I felt abandoned. There was no welcoming voice to soothe my fears; no teacher came alongside me to make me feel at home, and the children I was placed with were too young to make friendly conversation. The day wore on interminably and confusingly, and I went to bed that night and cried bitterly, lying awake for hours listening to the sounds outside the window. Would the taxi come and take me back after all?" I desperately willed it to come, and listened in vain for the sound of the wheels on the crunchy gravel.

There were all kinds of strange and frightening sounds in this lonely place. Even the wind seemed to be trying to get away as it whistled through the ventilators. I lay there listening to is two-toned howl, eerie and ghostly in the silence of the night. The ventilators tried to stop its escape. I noticed a 'click' and a low moan as the wind tried to force its way through, then as it tried harder, the pitch rose up in an agonizing wail until there was another 'click' and the wind gave up to build strength for another try. It seemed to be voicing all the forsakenness I felt.

I began to imagine it as a friend sympathising and putting into sound what I could not vocalise myself. As time went by, I was to build up a strong picture of what I thought the sky was like and what was going on outside. I used to dream that I had friends in the sky who would look down on me and share in my desolation. I charted a mental picture of the rise and fall of the wind, and came to notice that in September it began to sound more urgent, but in the spring it would be more capricious. The impressions grew and became very vivid and real.

Now and again on that first night I heard a strange noise within the room I was apparently sharing with other young children like myself. There would be a scuffling sound, followed by a careful scraping noise. It happened several times, and it was not long before I found out that it was the sound of the children getting out of bed and pulling their chamber pots out from under the beds!

In the morning I was to discover that our clothes were kept in a basket alongside the chamber pot. I was expected to fold my clothes neatly, and place them in thc basket, then I had to make my bed. It had to be done precisely. A maid instructed me:

"You must put this sheet on first," she said, and then she directed my hands to the bottom of the bed.

"It has to tuck in like this." She yanked my small frame to feel the smart mitred corners. I could hardly lift the mattress to force the sheet underneath. It was a very complicated feat to produce those impeccable corners. I could not understand why they were so important.

Then she put my hands to touch two blankets. "These two grey ones go next," she continued. They had a smooth feel, and I mentally joined 'grey' with 'smooth'. The impossible mitred corners were insisted upon once more. Then she made me feel another blanket. It was rough and hard.

"This brown one must go on top of the others." She went on making the bed as she spoke. I thought 'brown' must be a horrid colour to feel like that. Lastly a counterpane covered everything else.

This was the beginning of my 'tactile' understanding of colour. 'Brown' signified a rough feel, with 'grey' meaning smooth. Ever afterwards, colours began to take on different 'feels'.

I associated red with hot because when I did something wrong I was told my face went red. My mother had often told me not to touch the hot poker in the fireplace, so it became synonymous with danger. There was also a box on the hearth containing coal for the fire. I was told not to touch the coal either, because it would make my hands black and dirty. So black became a forbidding colour. This was reinforced because the night was black, and I suffered my worst fears at night.

Blue had two different aspects. It could be cold, because when I felt ill I was often cold, but it could also be a 'happy' colour, because when the sun was shining, the sky was blue. I heard people say that the day might turn out fine 'if there was enough blue to make a sailor a pair of trousers!' I began to wish I knew what made the weather fine and the sky blue, or what caused my friend the wind to blow.

Most of the time I liked green. It was the colour of the grass where, at my last school we played in good weather. I thought of it therefore, as restful. But it did have its sinister side too. The mould on bad food was apparently green, so it could not be entirely trusted as a colour.

There was to be not much sitting on grass here - only the girls had grass to play on, the boys were restricted to the tarmac area. There were, however, some large playthings available to us. A slide, which we called 'the chute' was a particular favourite, and although it was the cause of many a grazed knee, we spent a lot of time on it.

Another very popular toy was a train which went around the playground on a special track. It had pedals to make it move, and we liked to see how fast we could make it go. Some time later, an extension was added to the building, and a sand pit was included in the new area. I was not surprised when I learned that this popular playing place had been the idea of my favourite teacher, Miss Richardson. She seemed to have a better understanding of our needs than most of the other staff, and I came to depend on her a great deal.

At East Grinstead, the staff had tried to make up to us for the lack of love in our lives. They anticipated our needs and were untiring in their attention to the disadvantaged toddlers in their care. I soon realised that things were different here.

Breakfast was regulated and varied very little. On one day there would be porridge, on the next, two half slices of bread in warm milk. There was never any sugar. Following this, there might be a half slice of bread with Marmite - we were not allowed any more than one. On Sundays, if we were lucky, there would be cornflakes instead, which we used to call 'Post Toasties' for no apparent reason!

I soon got to know that there were maids to help us at the table. The one who was assigned to my group was called 'Dora'. Her first task was to tie on my bib, or 'feeder' as it was called. I used to feel her cold fingers on my neck.

At the end of the meal monitors would collect up all the feeders, and any that were too soiled to be used again would be sent to the laundry, but the rest remained to be handed out at the next meal - not necessarily to the same child!

Dinner in the middle of the day was the meal I came to hate most. It consisted of meat, potatoes and vegetables, but it was always completely bland and unappetising. The stew was worst of all. We could only imagine what it looked like, and I could never make out what the bits in it were.

Puddings were as bad. There was usually either rice, or tapioca which was sometimes thoughtfully dressed up with the addition of a currant or two; or maybe there would be steamed marmalade pudding. Whatever it was, it was either too stodgy to eat, or too watery.

Tea consisted of one half slice of brown bread and butter. If we wanted more we would put up our hands, and a half-piece of white bread would be given to us, but we could only do this twice. There was an absolute limit of three half slices. Sometimes there would be honey or jam, but only on Sundays would there be cake.

Some children received food parcels from home, but they were not allowed to keep the food to themselves. It had to be shared out with everyone - one cake would be divided between all fifty-six children!

We were obliged to eat everything we were given. Most of the time we did - no matter how much we disliked it, because there was not usually enough to fill us. But should any child refuse to eat, they would be severely punished.

Punishments were handed out for a variety of misdemeanours. A common punishment was to be 'off extras' for a week or two. This meant that we would be denied anything sent from home, and was a major catastrophe to most of us. Home was our link with love, and to be denied that slender bond was a severing of a vital life-line.

Corporal punishment was adhered to strongly by the staff as a necessary part of a child's upbringing. It would be meted out viciously to boys and girls alike with a large hair brush, or we could be whipped with a strip of wood kept for the purpose. All of this would, of course, be administered on bare bottoms.

And it was not only offenses like rudeness to staff, or fights with other children which brought retribution. We could incur a whipping for not drying our hands or behind our ears properly, and jumping on beds was also considered cause for a beating.

There were also undefined mistakes which we were unable to anticipate. One of these I learned one day when I was walking behind Matron in the corridor. I misjudged the distance that she was ahead of me and stepped on her heel. She turned on me angrily.

"You stupid child!" she shouted, "You need to learn to be more careful! Go straight to your bed!"

In terror, I knew what this would mean. I would have to put on my night-shirt - we were not allowed to wear pyjamas - and I would wait, shaking in fear for the inevitable. Some time later, at a convenient time for the staff member involved, she would be heard coming step by step up the stairs, nearer and nearer. She would march to the bed, rip down the bedclothes, and grab the offender by the ankles, thus holding him or her upside down so that the nightshirt fell down over the head, exposing a bare bottom. Then we would be beaten ruthlessly with the hair brush, finally to be left sobbing and bruised.

Another occasion which incurred me a beating was the result of a piece of mischief in the playground. In a weak moment, I saw that some fun could be had by placing a stone in a strategic place on the train track. I thought it would be fun to hear the train topple over when it hit the stone.

In mounting excitement, I listened to the rumbling sound as it moved closer, bringing the unsuspecting driver towards where I had placed the stone. I giggled in delight as it went over, but my laughs vanished instantly when I was grabbed angrily by a member of staff. With terror I realised that I was going to get a whipping. She dragged me into the boot room and ordered: "Take your trousers down." I heard the sound of the whipping wood being picked up and my heart stopped in fear.

"Don't want to," I murmured desperately, but in anger she forced me to comply, and the whipping was mercilessly applied.

The combination of loneliness, fear and desolation took its toll. We had to do as we were told during the day, but at night, after we had gone to sleep, our minds could not be ordered. Mine signalled its disturbance by causing my body to sleep walk. Many times I was found wandering about the school fast asleep. It seemed pointless to order me not to - I had no control over my unconscious actions.

There was to be a pleasant change coming into my life, however, and one night at bath time, Dora told me about it.

"There's a new boy coming to school," she said as she wrapped me in a towel.

This was interesting news. It would be nice to meet someone different.

"What's his name?" I asked.

"Joseph," Dora replied kindly, rubbing my legs.

Miss Richardson had told us Bible stories, and the name rang a bell.

"Like the boy with the coat of many colours?" I said, half in question and half thoughtfully.

"That's right," she answered as she helped me into my night shirt.

We became inseparable. Joseph was partially sighted, and became the real friend I had never had, and since he was very insecure, he was glad to have a companion too. It was to be the start of a life-long friendship.

Chapter 3

SHAPING THE FUTURE

There were four resident teachers at Harborne, and fifty-six children, so each teacher was responsible for fourteen children. Of the four, Miss Morley was assigned to the partially sighted children, and the rest were divided between Miss Janus, Miss Williams and the kindly Miss Richardson, who was my teacher.

Miss Morley was not liked by any of the children. She did not seem to be able to identify with blindness, and made no allowances for the fact that not only were her pupils blind, but they were children!

Although there was very little which stopped us from doing what we wanted to do, we were all rather obliged to take a little care when moving about, and part of our training consisted in learning to be reasonably cautious. Miss Morley, however, was a stranger to caution. She thundered about, charging from place to place like a hurricane, chivvying and bellowing at everyone, and pushing those who did not move fast enough.

Miss Richardson was my favourite teacher in spite of the fact that she was, like the rest of the staff, a believer in corporal punishment. My earliest experiences of a whipping were at her hand. It was difficult to equate this violent behaviour with the gentle, caring side of her character which we thankfully, saw more often. Someone once said 'Anger is the reverse side of the coin of love'. This perhaps describes, or to some degree explains the anomaly.

Most of the time she was gentle and kind, and fully understood the problems we faced both as children and in our sightlessness. She referred affectionately to us, the youngest children in the school, as 'little ones'.

"Forward, little ones," she would say as we led out of assembly in our straight , orderly lines, and 'come along, little ones," as we came back in from play.

Whenever we had to walk anywhere, it had to be in the close formation of the 'crocodile' - two by two, and holding hands. Joseph and I would always try to stay together, and before long we had established a routine which was broken only on Sundays when we had to go to church. Church, therefore, became doubly trying. It was not only incredibly boring, but it separated me from Joseph because he did not have to go like the rest of us. He, apparently, was something called a 'Catholic', and that meant he could miss the weekly ritual. I wished I was a 'Catholic' too.

We hated the services which were dull and unintelligible to children. The vicar droned on and on, oblivious to the fact that none of us understood, and indeed, he never ever referred to our existence. There was never a children's story or a song that we could sing and understand. We were totally ignored.

Miss Richardson, therefore, made up for the gap in our Christian education. Her morning assemblies became one of the times we looked forward to most. She taught us the songs which we loved to sing and were to remember ever afterwards. We sang with gusto:

'Wide, wide as the ocean,
High as the heavens above;
Deep, deep as the deepest sea
Is my Saviour's love!'

Then there was 'In my heart there rings a melody', and 'He did not come to judge the world, He did not come to blame'. My favourite was the less grammatical but very beautiful 'Jesus the Saviour is of boys and girls - none other ever could save boys and girls.' I think this was probably my first emotional experience of melody. I felt a surge of joy every time we sang it.

They were all lovely, and we built up a wealth of songs and hymns which would never be forgotten even though many children might not be church goers when they grew up.

But learning the hymns was not my only enjoyment during these lesson times. I was just as interested in the way Miss Richardson played the piano. It began from the moment we went into the room when she would get the key and turn it in the lock to open up the piano. I listened to the 'click' of the lock and the 'tap' as the cover went up, and waited in eager anticipation.

Then she would produce lovely sounds from that instrument which I longed to try to imitate. But we were never allowed to touch the piano. When our lesson ended, the cover went down, and the key turned once again. These times were welcome interludes in a rigorous and sometimes cruel routine.

My friend, Joseph, was a very insecure little boy. He had suffered the removal from his family to be sent away to school like the rest of us, and it affected us all in different ways. I sleep walked, but Joseph was a bed-wetter. There was only one way to deal with bed-wetters in this school, and in anguish for Joseph, I knew what would happen when the supervisor came in one morning to get us all up. Having inspected his bed, she shouted at him angrily,

"You dirty boy! How many times must I tell you not to do that?" Then she caught hold of his arm with one hand, and the large hard-backed hair brush with the other. My heart missed a beat as I listened helplessly to the sickening crack! crack! crack! of the brush on Joseph's bare bottom, and his terrifying screams as the brush rained down on him. When it was over, I sat next to him in friendly sympathy.

It was Joseph's turn to sympathize with me some time later.

After breakfast each morning, we all lined up to go to the playroom. The corridor sloped down towards he assembly hall which doubled as a gymnasium, and our playroom went off to the left. In a corner at the end of the corridor stood a fire extinguisher which we were frequently told to 'leave alone'. I was fascinated by this strange implement and wondered how it worked, although I did not dare to touch it. As we filed down the corridor and past the extinguisher one day, I must have inadvertently gone close to it.

"Leave that alone!" came the angry shout from the teacher, who at the same time yanked at my arm. In pulling me away, my sleeve caught on the extinguisher, and it fell to the floor, unfortunately pointing towards the open playroom door. Then I discovered what effect the extinguisher would have in the event of a fire.

It suddenly went off, showering children and playroom with a strong force of spreading foam reaching right to the limits of the room! Mayhem followed. Children screamed and gasped as the foam covered them all from head to foot, and people came rushing in to see what had happened. In the confusion, deafening noises met the ear - the rushing sound of escaping foam, the screams of the children, and shouts of the staff who desperately tried to stop the flow. The extinguisher would not be halted. It continued until it was empty. The devastation was complete.

As they dragged me away, Joseph was left to imagine the consequences and to helplessly await my return. I was 'off extras' for two weeks, and given the usual severe beating which I remember to this day.

Our lessons consisted mainly of three subjects. Learning Braille formed the greater part of the day's work, Scripture came next, and thirdly, Arithmetic. But before we started any work, Miss Richardson would lead us up the corridor to our classroom, making sure that we kept in a straight line as we walked. Once in our classroom, we had to stand behind our chairs ready for prayers.

"Quiet, little ones, now we must pray," Miss Richardson would say, and then she would add illogically, 'Hands together - and EYES CLOSED!" We never knew why she said it, but we complied obediently!

Then she would pray reverently to a Heavenly Father, talking to him as though she knew him intimately. Most of us either did not know or had forgotten our fathers, so we listened to her words with fascination. She prayed for the boys and girls in the sick bay, our parents and loved ones - this was added for those who had foster parents - and then she would pray for our lessons.

Years later, when I was to recount this memory, I would add that in my case I felt the time well spent, since my arithmetic was always mental, my fractions vulgar, and my decimals pointless!

Braille teaching was, of course, essential. It is a method of reading which uses raised dots in groups of up to six to form different patterns. Each letter is a different grouping of the dots, and first we learned the shape of each letter.

Later we were to learn that whole words could be formed by setting the patterns side by side, or that the process could be abbreviated by using one pattern for a whole word.

We learned using a wooden board with holes in it, into which pegs could be placed in the appropriate patterns, and it took most of us about three years to become completely fluent. I grew to love reading, and particularly enjoyed 'Aesop's Fables' and Enid Blyton stories.

We often had to read aloud during Scripture lessons, passing the book from child to child with a finger held on the spot where we stopped and the next would take over. Miss Richardson, however, would sometimes tell us the Bible stories, keeping us interested with her vivid descriptions of the amazing adventures from the pages of the Bible. She also encouraged us to memorise Bible texts, and gave prizes for those who learned the most. I proudly earned two different prizes, and received Braille copies of the Gospels of Matthew and Luke which I treasured for years.

For some children, these would be the only presents they would receive. Many of us came from very poor families, and some did not know their families at all, so birthdays and Christmas were often only marked with presents if a kindly member of staff gave one. My family remembered my birthdays, but I could only hope to receive a small gift. On my seventh birthday, my mother sent me a bar of 'Lux' soap, but I was not allowed to keep it. Matron decided it was of better use elsewhere.

Miss Richardson, however, did what little she could to make her children happy. She could not openly give us presents, but as I dressed on that birthday morning, I discovered something hidden amongst the clothes in the basket under my bed. I felt the unexpected shape and realised that it was a little mouth organ. Mouth organs were familiar playthings to us, but this one was for me personally, and I knew it must have come from Miss Richardson. I was overjoyed, and soon learned to play it well. It became a source of delight to me for many years.

She would also reward good work by handing out 'Dolly Mixture' sweets. If we did well, out would come the little rustling bag, and she would put a little sweet into our open hands. Those little treats were highly prized and we worked hard, not only for the reward, but because we loved our teacher.

Arithmetic lessons were carried out with the help of an ingenious mechanism called a 'Taylor Frame', but which we described as a 'Type Board'. It was constructed in such a way that we were able to do all kinds of arithmetical calculations in 'Maths Code'. It was a metal frame with a number of octagonal holes in it set on a wooden backing board. A tray on the right hand side held the 'type': these were small blocks of metal which had a bar projection at one end, and two points at the other. They were inserted into the octagonal holes, and numbers were represented depending upon the positioning of the 'type'. It had to be turned clockwise - the bar end rotating to produce 4,6, and 8 at the compass points North, East and South, with the odd numbers found by lifting the type out of the hole and replacing it at a twenty degree angle to the right and then rotating again.

The nine and the nought, together with the arithmetical signs, were produced by turning the 'type' over so that the two points could be placed into the octagonal holes, and the process repeated.

This method of teaching eventually was replaced because the

type was made of lead and the children would absent-mindedly suck it! Teachers and children were quite unaware of the dangers in those days, and we shall probably never know what problems this caused.

When we reached seven years of age we were allowed to join the 'cubs'. There was always great excitement when we joined this youngest section of the Boy Scout Movement, and Joseph and I wore our special jerseys with pride. Each week we would go to the meeting in the nearby Scout hut, and take part in as many of the activities as possible.

A special treat was to be able to play with the model railway that ran around the walls of the hut. There was always a great rivalry for a turn.

A highlight of the time we spent in the cubs occurred when the 78th Birmingham troop to which we belonged, was singled out for a particular honour. As far as we knew, we were the only troop in the country - and perhaps the world - specifically for blind boys, and we learned with delight that the leader and founder of the Boy Scout Movement, Lord Baden-Powell was coming in person to visit us.

It was a day to be remembered. We waited and listened in awe as the great man himself was met from his car by local dignitaries, with all the boys meticulously smart in their uniforms. Speeches were made and explanations given, but when they were over, the fun was really to begin. Lord Baden-Powell undoubtedly had a gift for knowing what boys would enjoy, for instead of 'standing on ceremony', he got down amongst us all and played the games we liked. He laughed and joked, joined in everything, and even got down on all fours and let us ride on his back! We found the day wonderful fun and very exciting.

Back at school, a new member of staff was appointed. Her name was Miss Penny, and as she was not a teacher but a supervisor, she was responsible for more of our out-of-school time. She soon became a favourite with the children, and had special 'pet' names for us all. Mine was 'Peterkin', and I was never afraid to hear her calling me, since she did not have the hard, formal tone which some of the others had. She was kind and thoughtful, and made little caring gestures, like slipping a fluffy toy dog or rabbit into our beds with us at night. To children who were deprived of a loving parent, and regimented in most of what they did, small touches such as this meant a great deal.

Joseph and I continued to spend a lot of time together, finding in each other's company a replacement for the brothers we hardly knew. If we could, we would commandeer the two donkeys on wheels in the playroom, and race each other across the room, trying to avoid obstacles.

"Mandy can go faster than your donkey!" I would shout in delight. We never knew why it was so called, but the other donkey was very soft and clean to the touch and was named extraordinarily, but aptly.

"Hygiene will beat you - you'll see!" Joseph shouted back as we raced across the room scattering bricks and balls in our path.

These, as well as most other toys in the playroom were given to the 'BRIB' by friends and well-wishers. There were a variety of toys there: prams, scooters, three-wheeled bikes, and for the bigger boys, a kind of trolley on wheels which they called 'coasters'. But there were also plenty of building or constructional toys like 'Meccano' or bricks to play with. I was particularly fond of a crane which could be wound up and made to pick up magnets.

Once each year, the playroom was the scene of a special get-together. It was called 'Doll and Mouth Organ' time, for the excellent reason that every child was annually given a present of a doll - for a girl, or a mouth organ for a boy. During a three year stay at the school, it would be possible, if you were careful, to acquire a set of three dolls or three mouth organs! No-one knew why this day had come about, and no-one knew either why only dolls and mouth organs were given. It was simply always done, and there was no more to be said! Ever since Miss Richardson had given me my special present of a mouth organ on my birthday, I had become good at playing it, and when Joseph got his, we would try to outdo one another at playing the loudest or best.

Other special occasions to be eagerly looked forward to were our visits to Dudley Zoo where we went to *hear* the animals. We could tell how large or small an animal was by the sound his paws or hooves made as he walked, and if he snorted or made a loud noise, we would shout back in delight.

The annual carnival was another time which could be guaranteed to take our minds off our work for a few days in anticipation of the fun to be had.

We could hardly wait for the afternoon to come when we would be allowed to stand at the roadside and be part of the noisy, chattering crowd as the procession passed by. We shouted and cheered, and Joseph and I clapped our hands in joy as the different floats passed by.

But even when it had all gone by, our fun was not entirely over, for we knew that the carnival procession would return back along the same route later, and we would hear it when we were in bed. It would be very late before we slept that night.

The usual three bedtimes for the different age groups were six o'clock, six-thirty, and seven o'clock, but at a quarter past nine, we would all be wide awake, waiting for the distant beat of the drum, and each of us longing to be the one to hear it first. The excitement mounted as the band got nearer and louder. We heard the distant bump, bump, bump of the drums before we heard anything else, and then soon the other sounds would become clear until they were passing at the closest point, and we would hold our breath in excitement until it all gradually died away again. It was all the more wonderful because it seemed to us that it was all happening in the middle of the night!

But the year I was seven saw the momentous event which eclipsed all others, and although I didn't realise it at the time, it was to set me up for life.

The day it happened was ordinary and dull. We had begun in the usual way with washing, breakfast, lessons - the rigid routine which we had always followed. I had no reason to suppose this day would be any different.

Our next activity was to be 'Choice', when we went into the playroom to choose what we would play with. I chose the rubber bricks, and began to build quietly by myself. To my surprise, Miss Richardson interrupted my play.

"Peter," she called, 'you must leave that now, you are going to learn to play the piano!"

I stopped with a brick in my hand, and tried to take in what she had said. 'Learn to play the piano', I repeated in my mind. Could she really mean that? It was the thing I had most longed to do ever since I had heard the first notes she had played to us in our singing lessons.

But we were never allowed to touch the piano. Surely she couldn't mean that I was to be allowed to turn the key, lift up the lid and make those lovely sounds?

"Come along, now," she continued, 'Mr. Clark is going to teach you this afternoon."

It was true! I really was going to learn how to play the piano. And this afternoon! This was wonderful! Mr. Clark was going to show me how to play just like Miss Richardson - this afternoon! Tomorrow perhaps she would let me play for the singing instead!

I was rather disappointed that at the end of the lesson, I had learned very little in my opinion. Mr. Clark, who was blind like us, began by teaching me the names of the notes and how to find them. We played 'Find the Note' games, which were fun, but I could see that the whole job was going to take longer than I thought.

I was given the 'Walter Carroll' book in Braille to practice with, and it was actually not really very long before I was playing simple tunes. My first exercise was called 'Very Sedate', and consisted of a few notes played with the right hand, and continued with some more with the left. Gradually I began to learn co-ordination.

Soon 'The Jolly Farmer' followed, and 'In the Quiet Wood', although by the way I played it, it would have more appropriately been called: 'The Herd of Elephants'!

My teachers soon admitted that they had chosen aright in my case. I learned and practised eagerly, savouring every moment I was allowed to spend at the beloved piano. My playing developed in leaps and bounds, and I knew that I was on the way to being able to play well.

When the holidays came I would be able to tell my mum and dad about the piano. I had an even greater reason for longing for the holidays.

Chapter 4

FAMILY PERFORMANCES

We went home three times each year. As the time came round we would be nearly beside ourselves with anticipation, and could hardly wait to go to the homes which had become so distant to us.

On the morning of our departure, the chatter in the washroom would be more animated than usual as each one would try to tell the others about what they hoped they would do at home. The sink was one continual trough with swinging bowls above it so that the water could be tipped out when we were finished. On these extra special days, there would have been less washing and more tipping if the maids had not been at our sides to see that nothing was neglected!

My real home was a different world. I had to get used to confined space instead of the lengthy corridors and dormitories of school; there were not as many toys as there were at school; there were comparative strangers instead of friends. I missed Joseph. Later on he was to come home with me occasionally, but at first I had to manage on my own and it felt very strange.

I had been away for about five years by now, apart from the holiday visits, and during these times I realised that I was really the stranger in a family of established children. My brother Harry, was by now twelve years old; my sister Lily, ten; and Marjorie was nine. They were all much too old to play with a seven-year-old like me, although they were always interested at first to find out how I got on and coped with things. Soon the novelty would wear off, and they would get on with more important things.

But my youngest sister, Betty, was another matter. She was only five, and was delighted to have someone to play with. We became great friends in the short times we had available, and I was glad to have someone to relate to at home.

My parents were, indeed, thrilled by the news that I was learning to play the piano. Unfortunately, we did not own such a thing, and as the holiday progressed, I realised how much I missed having one available to me. I wondered if I would forget what I had learned by the time I got back to school. My parents were concerned about the situation too. They decided to do something about it.

We discovered that the people over the road had a piano for sale. It was probably not advertised as such, but it was known that they needed money, and they were delighted to have something which was saleable. After some careful bargaining, the old piano was soon installed in our living room, and I was completely satisfied. A long time later we found a note inside it which revealed that if the people over the road did not pay something off their rent arrears, they were to be evicted form their house!

It did not score very highly in the good piano ratings, but I loved it. It became my refuge when the going was tough, my confidante when I had no-one to talk to, and my companion in joy. My ability to play it grew rapidly. The sacrifices made by my parents to acquire that old piano will never be known, but they must have been considerable. Life in the late thirties was not easy for most people, work was scarce, and my parents had known nothing but struggle.

My grandparents had been forced to go to great lengths in order to live. My father's mother had been left with several young children when her husband died, and she was obliged to consign them to a 'home'. Even though it was doubtful whether they warranted it, they were 'certified' and sent to a mental institution. One remained there for the rest of his life, visiting us now and again. He was allowed out for specific times, and used to enjoy his times with us. As the time came for him to return, he would reluctantly say 'I must go back or I'll get a 'towelling'!" I sympathised and understood his apprehension.

My mother's brother, Fred, was the family celebrity. He had a piano accordion which he played very well and from which he was inseparable. During the war he insisted on taking it to France with him, where, so family legend tells, it became the means of making him a hero.

The story goes that his platoon became surrounded by Germans, and were in danger of annihilation. But Uncle Fred saved the day. He picked up his trusty accordion, and began to play a selection of well-known German tunes. The Germans were enthralled and held off their attack while they listened. Uncle Fred kept on playing until reinforcements arrived, and they were all saved!

At one point I was given an eight bass accordion, and was assured that I took after Uncle Fred when I made up tunes on it! However, after the arrival of the piano, Uncle George, another of my mother's brothers, became the recognised source of my talent since he played the piano well, although could not read a note of music.

As my ability on the piano increased, so did my interest in music. My holidays became times of release when I could listen to any kind of music I liked. At school we were only allowed to listen to 'good' music. The popular kind was considered vulgar and to be avoided at all costs, and we only got to hear any if we pressed our ears to the staff room door!

At home we had an old valve wireless which I listened to avidly. I would sit in my favourite chair; turn the switch on the side of the wireless; wait for it to warm up, and then tune it in to any station transmitting music. I liked dance music best. There was the Victor Sylvester orchestra, Carol Gibbons, Charlie Kunz with his individual style of piano playing, and many others. I began to imitate them all, matching their various styles in my own playing.

Twice each day there would be a thirty minute block of continuous music on the wireless called 'Music While You Work'. I would play along with it, in this way learning all the pop songs. My dad encouraged me. He recognised a talent which could have substantial financial rewards.

Dad was the secretary of the local darts team at the 'Dog and Partridge' round the corner. Most evenings he would be heard to say 'I'm just going round the corner' - and we always knew which way his steps were bent. They were more bent on the way back!

It was the custom of the team to meet in someone's home for a late-night get together now and again. When I was home from school, dad would invite all his mates back to our house, where they would be wined and dined on meat and pickle sandwiches and mugs of tea - or beer if finances ran to it.

When they were suitably relaxed, he would come upstairs and wake me from what was, by that time, a sound sleep, and I would be brought downstairs to entertain the company. A dining chair would be put at the piano for me to sit on - we could not afford a piano stool - and I would play all the favourite melodies of the day while they all sang loudly. There would be choruses of 'If you were the only girl in the world'; 'I'll be your sweetheart; and 'It's a long way to Tipperary'.

Dad managed the whole production. He saw to it that they were sufficiently entertained, and then he would bring on the finale. This was a tenor to whom he would signal at the appropriate moment, and who would step forward and sing movingly 'He was only a poor blind boy'. As the hankies were brought out and sniffs were suppressed, the hat would be passed round.

There was usually a good collection, and Dad saw to it that I received my reward. His cut as manager had to be considered of course, and since it was an important job, he reckoned a 95% commission was reasonable. Once we got nine shillings and sixpence, and my portion was fourpence.

But my desire to entertain had been kindled.

I hated going back to school after the holidays. Just as I had got used to the relaxation of home and was getting to know my sister Betty, I had to give it all up and go back to the rigidity of school routine. I knew the time was getting near when my mother started getting my uniform ready - the horrible uniform which reminded her of the problem of school fees.

Most of the cost of our education was found by the BRIB, but families were expected to make a small contribution. Our clothes for school were obtained for us, but sooner or later a bill would arrive at home for the parental contribution. My parents could never manage it and it was a continual embarrassment. The authorities persisted, however, and my father paid the ultimate price - one night in Winson Green prison for debt. They never got the money, though, and in the end, the BRIB footed the entire bill.

My heart sank when I realised my mother was sorting my uniform out in preparation for school. I begged her to let me stay at home. I enjoyed playing with my sister Betty, and the informality of each holiday underlined the starkness of our lives at Harborne.

"Please don't make me go back," I pleaded. 'I promise I'll be good - I'll do anything you say - please don't send me away again!"

But it was no use. When the day came for my return, I cried bitterly, and clung to my mother. By way of consolation she gave me a little bag of raisins to eat on the way. They were so good, and such a life-line to home that I hardly dared to eat them. But they were no substitute for a loving family.

When I returned to school in September 1939, a new sound

met our inquisitive ears. Our school was situated near a barracks, and we began to hear the sounds of soldiers being prepared for war. The war had been declared on September the third, just before I had to come back to school, and we returned wondering what was going to happen.

The soldiers drilled most of the time, and at night we would lie awake and listen to the sounds of their feet as they marched about the parade ground. We noticed the way the shouted orders changed the pattern of the marching. It seemed urgent and foreboding. We fell into an uneasy sleep.

The days following the outbreak of the war were filled with apprehension. It was clear that something terrible was expected to happen, and we waited nervously to discover what it was to be. It was not a long wait.

One morning there was a feeling of action in the air when we woke up. We had already realised that not all the children had returned to school. Some had been allowed to remain at home and we wondered why this should be. I wished I could have been one of them.

Our belongings were collected together, and it was obvious that we were going somewhere. We soon found out that we were to be sent away from the Birmingham area because it was thought that the Germans would be dropping bombs here first.

Soon a large furniture van drew up at the front door of the school and nine of us were ushered out and into the back of it for a journey to 'somewhere safe'. My apprehension was heightened when I realised that although I was to be included in the nine, Joseph wasn't.

Our safe haven was to be a large house called Bockleton Court at Tenbury Wells on the borders of Herefordshire and Worcestershire, to where the senior girls from Edgbaston had already been taken. The nine of us who joined them were those whose homes were considered to be in the most vulnerable areas around Birmingham and Coventry. The others who had not returned to school apparently lived in lower risk areas.

To our surprise the change proved to be very much for the better, and here began a completely unexpected time of fun and relaxation.

To start with we were 'adopted' by the girls to be fussed over and indulged in everything. They were supposed to be our supervisors - making sure that we made our beds correctly and performed all our chores, but they spoiled us dreadfully, and waited on us hand and foot.

One of their tasks was to cut our bread and butter very thinly, explaining that this was part of the 'saving' for the war effort. Perhaps it was because they had known shortages themselves in the past and therefore knew how hungry we were, but they did not try very hard at 'saving', and so made everything a game.

It seemed as though the prospect of war had been pushed into the background for the time being. There were no bombs falling - not here or anywhere - so we all relaxed in our new and friendly surroundings.

It was only the staff who showed any signs of nervousness, and who seemed to be waiting for something to happen before they could organise any lessons. We, therefore, had nothing to spoil the idyllic autumn days. We laughed, played, had picnics and began each glorious day by running out into the orchard to pick an apple from the trees to eat before breakfast!

The older girls were not my only friends, however. I was soon to become a special favourite of 'The Colonel' who was the owner of Bockleton Court. Colonel Prescot lived nearby and often dropped in to see the youngsters who were occupying his old family home. He seemed to enjoy our company and we certainly looked forward to seeing him.

"Come on, then," he would say jovially, patting his knee, and I would climb willingly onto the large lap. "I know what you want!" he would laugh, and then he would allow my hands to go straight for his waistcoat and the chain that dangled across it. I would follow the chain through until I reached the pocket, and then feel for the watch inside. I was quite fascinated by that watch. I loved to feel its heaviness and smooth shape, and then, of course, I would put it to my ear so I could listen to its wonderful tick.

One day the Colonel sought me out especially.

"Here", he said, "I've got something for you. I thought you might like this". He took my hand and placed something in it. I felt it all over with rising excitement. I knew what it was straight away.

"It's only an old one, you understand", added the Colonel, "but you can have it to play with if you like."

I held the watch lovingly in my hands, savouring its comfortable shape, and could not believe it was for me. I held it to my ear, but it did not tick straight away. I shook it, and then to my delight, the ticking began! It went on ticking for a while before stopping again, but a shake would set it off every time. I was overjoyed with it, and kept it as a special treasure. Sometimes I would let the other boys feel it and listen to the tick, but they knew it was mine, only mine, and being rather jealous they left me to it.

Now and again one of the staff would take us to the little village school in Bockleton. There were just fifteen children in the school, so we were greeted with enthusiasm and spoiled here too! When the time came to leave Bockleton, each of the children wrote us a little appreciative letter.

We cried bitterly when we left. Depression hung over the Court during the last week when we had been told we would be leaving to go to another home in the country which had been found by Miss Richardson. Even our older 'supervisor' friends could not avoid shedding tears, and we avowed to each other that we would keep in touch. It was not until thirty-two years later that I was to meet one of those girls again.

Our next destination was to be a large house in the village of Wolverley near Kidderminster. The same nine children were the first to take up residence, and we tried to resume the idyllic lifestyle which we had come to enjoy at Bockleton. For a time we were not disappointed. There were still no lessons, and no apparent signs of war. Food, however, was not abundant, and we settled back into the routine of porridge one day, bread and milk the next. We knew it was being prepared when we smelled the phosphorus of the matches and heard the 'bump' as the gas fire burst into life.

We were gradually joined by some of the other children as they were allowed to return to the 'safe' school, but Joseph was not among them. We were also joined by a new matron. The 'grape vine' soon spread the news that the previous one had been dismissed for cruelty.

This new one brought an air of mystery. At a time when we were learning that all foreigners were suspicious, and that strangers could be 'fifth columnists' - or spies - we were instantly on our guard when we realised that Matron could speak German! She made no attempt to hide the fact, and openly greeted us with "Guten morgen!" or "Dankerschoen", if we held a door open for her. We were horrified, and quite certain that she was a German spy. Neither were we at all surprised when she proved to be every bit as cruel as the last matron. It was only to be expected from a Nazi in 1940.

As the school routine settled down, another disaster was to affect me perhaps more than some of the others. My favourite teacher, Miss Richardson, left. I mourned that there would no longer be anyone to understand my needs and give a kind word now and again. And I would not be able to hear her play the piano. I would miss those times dreadfully, and my loneliness drew me closer to the piano which became my only confidante.

Chapter 5

SHATTERED ILLUSIONS

My new piano teacher was Miss Colquoun. There were two pianos at Wolverley. One was in the conservatory, but the better one was in Miss Francis's room. I was beginning to be a little discerning where pianos were concerned, and appreciated the lighter touch and tone of the better piano. Miss Francis's room was also the one with the squeaky floor. All my lessons began with the squeaking of the floorboards as I walked across to seat myself on the stool.

Although Miss Colquoun was assigned to teach the earlier stages of playing the piano, she soon recognised in me the ability and willingness to compose my own melodies. She encouraged this vigorously by composing tunes especially for me and urging me to do the same. They were written down in Braille music, a complex notation based on the usual six dots, but which enabled me to fix and improve my compositions once I had grasped it. One of her special tunes written for me was called 'Rain and Sunshine', and through it she demonstrated that different moods could be achieved in the music. I followed her lead eagerly, and began to learn how to put a composition together as she showed me also how to add accompaniments to melodies. The bond between us became stronger, and we were to remain friends for a long time.

Music figured quite prominently at Wolverley as Miss Colquoun developed a percussion band in addition to her piano teaching. This drew all the children together in music making.

I had to play a tambourine, but I didn't like it very much. I preferred to play the piano.

The war, however, was building up and we soon came to realise that we were not as safe as we thought. A bomb fell on Kidderminster just one mile away from our school. Where could we find protection?

Beneath the building was a huge cellar where the dynamo which generated the electricity for the house was situated - for we were not on mains electricity here in Wolverley village. The cellar now became an extension of our living accommodation, to where we were shunted quickly at the sound of the air raid siren. It was equipped with mattresses, but it was cold, damp, fumy, and not very comfortable. It took some time too, to get used to the continual hum from the dynamo and the smell of the paraffin which fuelled it. Still, we felt ourselves to be safer there, so no-one complained.

There were two other teachers involved in teaching music at this time. One was Mr. Clark who taught the more advanced piano pupils, and the other was a Mr. Whitton who came in to school once a week to take community singing. We always knew when he had arrived because the smell of his cigarette smoke pervaded the whole building.

Mr. Clark showed interest in my progress although he was not my teacher. He must have been impressed with my performance because once he put a hand on my shoulder and said:

"One day, Peter, you will be famous. Then you won't want to be called 'Peter Jackson' any more - you'll call yourself 'Petrov Jacsonievitch'!"

Mr. Whitton's lessons were always popular. We learned all the old folk songs like 'Dashing Away with the Smoothing Iron', and 'D'ye Ken John Peel?', and sang them all lustily, but lessons were all occasionally punctuated by the siren and the race for the cellars.

Air raids were now not only expected during the night, they could come during the day, and an air of ominous suspense hung over us most of the time.

It was considered important that we got plenty of fresh air. To this end we were required to take frequent and long walks. Some of the walks had a purpose in that we visited something, and one of these was a tour round the local paper mill. Wood was unloaded there from the River Severn to be pulped and made into paper. The smells were fascinating, and if it had not been for the hunger, we would have loved it. But we were constantly hungry.

The war could not be entirely blamed for our lack of food. I knew hunger before the war - it seemed part of the school's method of avoiding 'gluttony' - but here at Wolverley we were desperately hungry all the time. Meals were sparse and unappetising; we got up from the table always wishing there was more, and our walks only served to fuel an appetite which was never satisfied. In fact, the walks became synonymous with hunger because they usually took a route to the village of Cookley where there was a bakery. As we approached the village, the smell of baking bread met us with agonizing strength. We would fall silent as each child breathed in the captivating smell as though it might fill the empty void in our stomachs. The walks became feats of endurance which left us weak, tired and ravenous.

It was strange that having taken so much trouble to protect us from the main threat of the bombs, we were then sent home in the summer. I returned gratefully to my home in Birmingham, and enjoyed the luxury of reasonable meals.

I found my family in a state of upheaval. They were all poorly for a start, and attempts had also been made to have my sisters evacuated to the country along with all the other children in high-risk areas. My mother gave up in the end, however, the girls simply would not go, and my youngest sister, Betty, cried and clung on so desperately that she could not be separated from mother.

So we stayed together throughout the summer until August 16th. On that morning my mother called the doctor. It was clear that something was wrong, and he soon diagnosed that all of the children had Scarlet Fever. An ambulance was called and we were all taken to Little Bromwich Isolation Hospital.

We arrived at six o'clock in the evening, and my brother and I were put in the same ward. We were given a bowl of soup, and then put to bed. A big, horrible rough blanket was then thrown across each bed to stop any flying glass caused by bombs, and we relaxed into an uneasy sleep.

Through the delirium of illness I heard the 'bleep-bleep' of crickets caught in the heating system, and the drone of aircraft in the sky above, with the occasional heart-stopping crash of bombs falling nearby.

As I began to get better, I became aware of the other patients in the ward - all men who spent their time listening to the wireless, keeping up with the fortunes of the war. Often they would tune in to Germany, from where the sinister voice of William Joyce could be heard broadcasting propaganda aimed at demoralising his British compatriots. He came to be called 'Lord Haw-Haw', and his nasal sounding voice introducing 'Germany calling! Germany calling!' sent shivers down the spine, but did little more to break the British spirit.

Near the hospital was a railway marshalling yard and a BSA motorbike factory, which had been taken over and was now used for making munitions. This was, of course, a prime target for the enemy, together with the adjacent Coventry area, and it was soon clear that they were concentrating their efforts here.

In silent fear, we lay listening to the deafening noise of anti-aircraft guns, the wail of the sirens, and the throbbing of the two-stroke engines of the planes going overhead. At the same time, we knew that the sickening thuds and explosions meant that buildings were being destroyed and people killed all around us. We waited for it to happen to us.

On one night, fifteen bombs fell in the hospital grounds. One hit the nurse's home and two nurses were killed. I was put into my brother's bed for comfort, and our dad, who came to visit us said:

"Don't worry, boys - I haven't given them our address!" But they did find us.

With a huge thud which seemed to reverberate around our heads, a time-bomb fell directly outside our ward door. Our hearts almost stopped as we realised that although we were still alive, we would all be killed if the bomb finally went off. A bomb disposal team were rushed in, and they dealt with it as we waited with bated breath. Relaxing later, we discussed the fact that if the bomb had not been on a delayed fuse, none of us would have survived.

When the day came for me to be discharged from hospital, I was sent back to school, but I had to remain in quarantine for a time. Unfortunately, the only place available which was away from the other children was Matron's room, and a bed was set up for me there.

It was like being sentenced to solitary confinement in prison. I could not mix with any of the children, of course, so I had no-one to talk to. There was only the occasional visit from a maid to work in the room or bring food on a tray, and I was left to consider my position in the room of a possible German sympathiser whom everyone thought was a spy!

There was nothing to do except wait for the next meal. They were not worth waiting for. Having been looked after and fed well in the hospital, I now went back to sparse school meals which left me, once again, permanently hungry. I lay in the lonely room with my thoughts, remembering the days when Joseph was around to play with; the holidays at home when I could play the piano for my dad's mates; and the kind Miss Richardson whom I missed so much.

When morning came, my empty tummy would long for the meagre breakfast of unsweetened porridge or bread and milk, and I devoured it quickly when it arrived.

A little later my nose began to detect a delicious smell wafting up from the kitchen. The kind of smell experienced very infrequently in these days of war shortages. It got stronger until my tummy began to rumble again, and my mouth water. It was unmistakably the smell of bacon cooking! I could hardly believe it. Bacon! Was it possible that I could be having more breakfast because I had been ill? Footsteps came nearer and my heart began to beat faster. The door handle turned and Matron walked into the room. Without a word, she walked over to the table and sat down. Almost immediately a maid followed her into the room and the tantalizing smell became intoxicating. I turned instinctively and eagerly towards her, but she did not come in my direction. She went straight to the table and I heard the sound of a tray being set down.

"Thank you", said Matron, briefly, and picking up the cutlery she began to eat. She had bacon and eggs, and I also heard the crunching sound of a knife slicing through toast.

I was crushingly disappointed. I was so desperately hungry. I lay there, my senses trying to shut out the sounds and smells of the delicious meal denied to me, and I was unspeakably lonely.

Going home for Christmas in 1940 proved something of a milestone. School Christmas celebrations began several weeks before the end of term, and by the time we went home we had usually had the school play, the carol service, Christmas dinner (such as it was) and received a present each.

At home, the whole thing began again. There were still all these wonderful things to experience, and I loved every minute.

This particular year brought much discussion about Father Christmas himself. My brother, Harry, at fourteen, humoured the rest of us. He knew. My eldest sister, Lily, at twelve, also knew, but would rather not know! Marjorie was eleven, and had her suspicions, but clung on to the hope; whilst myself and my younger sister, Betty, were totally convinced that Father Christmas was real, and that they all diced with danger to suggest that he wasn't!

It was all so exciting! Our mother managed to get us a few packets of paper chains, which we put together with much hilarity, and the old box of well-worn decorations was brought out, the contents sorted, straightened out and put up. In the fun and anticipation of the season, we almost forgot that there was a war on.

On Christmas Eve, we went to bed excited, our hearts beating fast, and with no hope of going to sleep. Dad went for his usual walk 'round the corner', which we all knew to be a visit to the 'Dog and Partridge', and Mum tried to get some last minute jobs done so that she could rest the next day.

It was late when Dad returned, and we had drifted into a shallow sleep. Mum was ready for bed, but waited up because there was still one important task to perform. She gave Dad the various packages, fruit and nuts which would be our presents, and he was to distribute them to the right beds.

Unfortunately his sojourn at the 'Dog and Partridge' had rendered him a little weak, and he picked his way unsteadily up the stairs. Half-way up, his legs gave way and he fell with a heavy thud, accompanied by some surprisingly well-articulated language which could probably be heard two streets away! Frantically, he tried to hold on to the presents, but lost control of the oranges, apples and nuts which bumped spectacularly back down each stair to the bottom with a variety of fascinating thumps, bangs and clatterings!

In a moment, heads appeared round the bedroom doors, aghast that Father Christmas should utter such words, and all of us half afraid that a bomb had fallen through the roof. Some of us would have preferred a bomb to the sight which met our eyes, for instead of Father Christmas, we saw Dad in a heap at the bottom of the stairs, liberally sprinkled with nuts and fruit! Our fragile belief in the wonderful figure of Father Christmas had been shattered once and for all!

The summer of 1941 was to be our last in the depressing surroundings of Wolverley before going up to the senior school, and one final incident was to round off our unhappy memories of the place.

It began with promise when we were given the opportunity

to 'adopt' a lamb from the nearby farm. One of the staff thought that it would be good for us to take a hand in caring for the little creature, and we entered into the project with a great deal of excitement and enthusiasm.

We called the lamb 'Frisky', and there was a lot of rivalry as to who was to feed it, stroke it and even to clean out its living quarters in the conservatory. For a time we could hardly concentrate on our lessons in the next-door classroom as we heard Frisky bleating for his bottle, and we cared for him tenderly.

Each day, he would be put on a lead and taken for a walk - just like a pet dog, and he caused quite a stir amongst the local inhabitants.

Sadly, however, there were those who seemed to begrudge the children their pet. For no apparent reason, one day during one of his walks, a group of louts set upon the defenceless lamb, and threw stones at him until they had killed him.

We were all completely devastated. It was such a senseless, cruel act. No-one could understand why it could have happened, and it left us bereft and desolate. We had all lavished our pent up love and emotions on the little lamb, and once again we had been thwarted. Many tears of sorrow and frustration were shed, and it was to become indelibly etched on all our memories for ever afterwards.

Years later when I studied the Scriptures, I felt an acute sympathy with Jewish children in the sacrificing of the Passover lamb each year. I reasoned that often the lamb would have been familiar to the family for a long time, perhaps from its birth, and there must have been many tears when the lamb was sacrificed. I knew just how they must have felt.

And so my days at Wolverley ended with characteristic melancholy.

Chapter 6

MIXED EMOTIONS

The summer had ended for us in sadness, and the autumn did not promise much relief. On Wednesday, October the 29th, I was transferred with the others to the senior school at Kinlet Hall, near Bewdley, Worcestershire.

I was never to understand why I transferred at the age of ten, whilst all the others were eleven. Presumably the staff thought I could cope with the change, and I was at least glad to get away from Wolverley.

Kinlet Hall was a large eighteenth century building with a drive nearly a mile long. The drive became something of a talking point to us eventually, because anyone new to the school always seemed to fall over on it. It was made of stone, and was presumably uneven in places, causing the unwary to trip and graze a knee on the rough stone. It just seemed as though falling was inevitable sooner or later.

Although experience had taught me that one could not expect too much of any change in circumstances, at least I was looking forward to being reunited with Joseph again. He was older than I and had transferred the year before. With all the upheavals caused by the war and illness, I had not seen him for a long time, and we greeted each other with delight. I did not know at the time, but Joseph was not to complete his education with the BRIB because it was decided that he had 'too much sight'. Eventually he had to leave, but for a time, however, it was good to renew our friendship, and he was to provide us with many hours of happiness on a quiet evening as he read to us from our favourite books. Joseph, therefore, showed us all around and helped us to settle in.

It all began interestingly enough. On the first Saturday, November the first, a Punch and Judy show was put on for us, although I did wonder why this kind of entertainment was given to an audience of mostly blind children! But it was not long before the full rigour of a Kinlet Hall routine became known. One of the first things we discovered was that food was even more scarce here than it had been at our previous schools. If we had been permanently hungry before, we were now often starving.

It did not help matters to learn that we were obliged to go on a walk of about four miles long every Saturday afternoon. The drive itself was nearly a mile, so this made our walk two miles without the two more miles which constituted the actual walk. It not only gave us a ravenous appetite, but we had to wait an extra hour and a half for the meagre tea. This was because the older children had privileges, one of which was that they were allowed out on Saturday afternoons until six-thirty. Since tea was usually at five, we had to wait the interminable hour and a half until they all returned. It was an incredibly long time in our desperation for food, and we hated it.

Saturday was also the day when we were given a sweet ration. Each child was given exactly three ounces of sweets - a bit of slab toffee, or maybe fruit sweets from a large tin; and most children devoured them in minutes. I liked to make them last as long as possible, however, savouring every taste to the end. It was dangerous to take them to church though, because any child caught crunching would be made to write out a psalm in punishment!

The term wore monotonously, and we began to look forward to the Christmas holidays which would begin on December the eighteenth. Spirits always ran high as the great time approached, and on the thirteenth, I was having a friendly tussle with another boy when I fell heavily on my arm.

It was soon diagnosed that I had fractured my wrist, and although I was in a lot of pain, I was extremely glad to miss the dreaded Saturday walk. I was taken to the nearby town of Cleobury Mortimer where the lady Doctor Fellowes gave me injections and reset my wrist with a splint. Back at school I was placed illogically in isolation in the sick bay! But Christmas was nearly here, and I would soon go home.

To my horror, with everyone else packing excitedly, I was informed that I could not go home. I was devastated. I had been looking forward so much to the holiday, it seemed too cruel to keep me at school just because I had broken my wrist. Surely I could manage at home just as well - perhaps better - than I could here?

It was not until February that I was to discover that my mother had been taken into hospital for major surgery, and that my wrist injury had nothing to do with the reason for staying at school. No-one saw fit to explain any reason why I was to remain. I was simply allowed to believe it was my foolishness in falling and bringing the problem upon myself.

For one reason and another, there were other children who had to stay at school over the holidays, and as soon as the main body of children had left, I was allowed out of isolation to join in the celebrations. And amazingly, we did have celebrations.

From the austerity of the usual term, we were pleasantly surprised to discover that a good time was to be had over Christmas. For a start there was more food. It was wonderful to feel reasonably full after a meal, and we livened up considerably at this welcome surprise.

But then we realised by the pervading smell of cigarette smoke that Mr. Whitton was to remain with us over Christmas. He was apparently in charge for the time, and we enjoyed his programme of entertainments; one of which was to play us the opera 'Hansel and Gretel' by Humperdink. I loved the music, and it became one of my favourites. We began to relax.

The whole time was, in the event, a very enjoyable one to our complete surprise, and it even included Christmas presents which we had not expected, and with which we were delighted. Deep down I was hurt that I had been denied the usual visit home, and every now and again I felt a pang of sadness, but the time was not a totally unhappy one.

Before the others returned at the end of the holiday, we were to have a visit to the chapel at nearby Chorley, where a children's party had been arranged and we were all invited.

Here I met Mr. Tolley, a delightfully genial man with a friendly Midlands country accent who seemed to take to me in particular. His daughter, Joan Stubbs, eventually became one of our dinner supervisors, and I was to see a lot more of the family before too long.

The principal of the school was Mr. Williams who was actually a very kind man. In fact, he was perhaps too kind, since he could always be relied upon to punish any misdemeanour with the words "Go to bed at six!" This would have been valid if we had ever obeyed the command but we simply avoided any compliance, and he was too gentle to enforce obedience. It was not surprising then, that he was privately referred to by us all not as Mr. Williams, but as Mr. "Go-to-bed-at-six"! We liked him, however and appreciated his kindness.

A story about Mr. "Go-to-bed-at-six" circulated, and amused us all. It concerned a visit he made to a conference of teachers of the blind in Germany before the war.

Apparently he had a room on the top floor of a hotel, and as he descended in the lift one day, it stopped at each floor to let someone in.

"Morgan", politely greeted each new addition to the lift.

"No - 'Williams'"! he responded, baffled.

In spite of his ineffectual discipline, and his rather vacant manner, he was undoubtedly an intelligent man who tried to give the school a family atmosphere. With three daughters of his own, he was used to family life, and knew what children needed. He made some attempt to make up to us for our loss in this respect in a number of ways, one of which was to read to us on Sunday nights. We loved these times and looked forward to them avidly.

He read all the children's classics to us: 'Moby Dick', 'Biggles', 'Supertramp' and many others. We also knew that about half way through a reading, he would pause to create a kind of interval, and would hand out 'mint imperials' to his delighted audience.

In February I was finally allowed home, due to the kindness of Mr. Williams who sympathised that I had not seen my family for so long.

My mother had recovered form her operation by this time, and I was overjoyed to see her, and grateful to Mr. Williams for allowing the visit mid-term. I was amazed, and somewhat relieved to discover the real reason why I had been kept at school, and although I was concerned for my mother, I was glad that it was not simply vindictiveness that had stopped me from coming home.

Mr. Williams was not altogether successful in his endeavours to provide a happy school, however. Other members of staff counteracted what they probably saw as too much indulgence, and were not so kind to us. After the relaxation of Christmas, everything returned to the normal austerity, and we began to wonder if we had dreamed it all.

Tea would consist of a wad of cheese on a piece of bread, with an occasional slice of bread and ham. It never filled us, and we were constantly hungry. Our only hope was to try to persuade the older boys to bring us back something to eat from the local bakery, on their permitted trips to the village. It we were lucky we might get a piece of malt loaf, or even a jar of meat paste to spread on our next available piece of bread for a change. It was a help, but never enough.

The war dragged on. We tried to keep up with what was happening, and rejoiced at every sign of advantage. At the news of success at Alamein, one of the boys slipped out of school and ran down to the church where he took the unprecedented step of ringing the bells. This was only supposed to be done in the event of an invasion, and even then, certainly not by one of our boys, but bells were being rung all over the country, and he wanted to be part of the excitement.

The vicar, however, who may have been disturbed from one of his frequent visits to the 'Eagle and Serpent', was not amused. He never understood boys. They were only useful for one thing - pumping the organ - and you had to make sure they did that properly! He never made any attempt to gear his services to their needs. The ringing of the bells was probably the most interesting thing that ever happened in that church!

If I had not been able to go home for Christmas in 1941, in 1942 I was not able to return to school after the holidays - in fact - I nearly didn't ever return there or anywhere ever again!

I went home drained and weak, but looking forward to some good meals and the excitement of the season. Christmas was fun, but I did not regain my strength and a return to school on January the eleventh loomed ahead ominously. Going back to school would be bad enough, but there was to be a Sunday School party on the ninth and I did not want to miss that. I used to look forward to Sunday School whenever I was home on holiday. I had made friends there, and I loved the singing and the stories.

One morning I awoke with a terrible pain. Mum sent for the doctor who diagnosed pneumonia. He prescribed some tablets which I took and which immediately made me sick. But by the end of the next day I was running a temperature, and the doctor was sent for again. This time he called an ambulance and I was whisked off to hospital for an emergency operation at 11.00 pm, for Peritonitis. The feel of the mask and the smell of the chloroform were to be the last things I remembered for some time, for the operation, (performed appropriately enough by a surgeon called Mr. Gore!) was to be only the start of it all. After the operation, if I had not actually had pneumonia before, I developed it then, with the addition of an abscess on the lung. I was desperately ill.

For some time I hung between life and death. A second operation was considered because there was so much poison throughout my system, but decided against.

The kind Mr. Williams even travelled the considerable distance to the hospital to visit me, bringing all sorts of goodies, but I was too ill to eat.

One Wednesday, my parents were summoned to my bedside and warned "He's sinking." My Uncle Jim, by way of trying to comfort them said:

"It's a blessing in disguise, really. He would never make much, anyway!"

We did not know at that moment, but the folk from my Sunday School had set up an hour of prayer for me between eight and nine o'clock that night.

It was at nine o'clock that I reached for the headset over my bed in order to hear the news. I felt a bit irritated because I had missed Victor Sylvester's Dance Club. I was totally unaware that the family were all waiting round my bedside for my last gasp! They were staggered! A miracle had happened! It was quite clear that God had not finished with me yet!

I began a slow improvement, remaining in hospital for the next ten days, during which time the staff tried to tempt me to eat.

"What would you like to eat?" they asked, 'anything at all - what do you fancy?' It was an offer I would have liked to have heard many times, but I could not do justice to it at that moment!

I was overwhelmed by the kindness I received. Even Nurse Stockwell who changed my dressings would try to soften the task by saying cheerfully:

"It'll all be done in two shakes of a bee's wing!"

Others heard of my miraculous recovery and visited me. Ladies from the local grocery store came and delightedly announced,

"He's a real grave-cheater!"

65

I came out of hospital on March 3rd, weighing two-and-a-half stones, at the age of eleven. Having been in bed for so long, I could hardly walk, and the pain in my feet was excruciating. I was going to have to gradually get my feet back into working order with exercise, and spend the time until then in a wheelchair.

It took a great deal of effort to get into the ambulance which was to take me home, and then when we arrived, the getting out was hampered by the excited welcome from our little dog 'Ruff', who bounded right into the ambulance to greet me! Ruff had been the only survivor from a bombed house, and had been found amongst the rubble by my brother. He brought him home, and between us we had nursed him back to health again.

Now he anxiously followed as I was half-carried into the house and placed in a chair. Ruff settled himself at my feet, to remain there until I could get around more easily, and then to follow me about in the wheelchair which I was obliged to use for a time.

I returned to school on March 13th, but there was to be a surprise waiting for me. As I sat in a chair by the fire, my friend, Joan Stubbs, came and sat beside me.

"Do you remember my parents, Mr. and Mrs. Tolley, whom you met at the Christmas party?" I nodded. They were kind, jolly and fun. I couldn't forget them.

"Well, you're going to stay with them to convalesce for a while. How do you feel about that?"

I was greatly relieved. I did not feel in the least able to begin the regime of school, and I liked the Tolleys very much. It would be nice to spend some time with them.

Chapter 7

NEW INTERESTS

In typically committed Christian style, the Tolleys named their home 'Ebeneezer Cottage' 'Ebeneezer' meaning 'Hitherto has the Lord helped us'. It was homely and comfortable - even though there was no inside toilet. This was to be found down the garden and past the pig sty!

I was to spend five weeks with the Tolleys, who did all they could to make my stay as enjoyable as possible. It was wonderful to have good, wholesome food, and to feel full after a meal, although it did not take much to fill me - I had been too used to scanty meals.

There were all sorts of interesting things to do. The Tolleys had lots of friends in the village, and all of them knew that they had taken in a sick, blind boy. They often took me on visits where I was unashamedly spoiled and fussed over.

Then there were the Thursday outings to Kidderminster on the bus, and chapel on Sundays where I went to Sunday School and also played the harmonium for the services.

The harmonium was an old instrument which had to be pumped with the feet. I found it very difficult at first, all the muscles of my feet having been out of action in hospital for so long. The pain was great, but I persevered, and it gradually became more easy.

The local doctor called to see me every day and was amazed at the way my feet were improving.

"What are you doing to this boy, to make this wonderful

change?" he asked the Tolleys. At first they could not think, then suddenly it dawned on us all.

"It's playing the organ!" they cried. 'It's no easy task, that - pumping continually with the feet, up and down throughout the hymns."

"Finest exercise possible!" laughed the doctor. 'No wonder his feet are improving!"

As I experienced the unselfish love of the Tolleys, I began to understand more and more about their simple faith. At Sunday School I learned about a God of love who, as Jesus, came to earth to take the punishment for the sins of every person in the world - including me. The Tolley's love of God began to make sense, and I realised that God loved me too. I enjoyed the services even more when I came to understand what God had done for me.

In spite of not seeing my family until the summer, I thoroughly enjoyed my stay with the kind Tolleys, but it all had to end eventually. In May I was to return to school.

The spartan regime of Kinlet Hall was all the more of a shock after my pleasant time at 'Ebeneezer Cottage'. Food was once again scarce, and staff could be ruthlessly cruel.

Each morning we would go to the washroom where there was a huge cylinder of hot water, but which did not hold enough water for everyone. If we were early, there was no problem, but if we were delayed, there would be only cold water left. So the first thing we did was to feel the tank to see if we were going to get a warm wash or a cold one.

After washing, we had to line up in the courtyard - rain or shine - for inspection, and we were required to wash according to the standard of the supervisor. If he decided we had not washed sufficiently well, then 'measures' would be taken.

One morning he decided that my partially-sighted friend, Eric, had not washed properly. He said he could see a 'tide mark' around his neck. Eric protested, and in doing so, he took the unfortunate step of raising his fists in frustration. The supervisor lowered his voice menacingly.

"Right. After breakfast we will settle the matter. We'll take our coats off."

The fourteen year old Eric knew perfectly well what that meant. He was to be engaged in a fist fight with the supervisor, from which there could only be one outcome.

The hall was an impressive room with marble pillars. In we all filed, and we had to watch as Eric was made to fight in a spar boxing match with the supervisor who attacked him mercilessly.

There was not much that Eric could do, and before long he was lying bruised, bloodied and breathless on the floor. With a final bellowing, the supervisor made it clear that Eric was never to put his fists up to him again.

I had, by now, another good friend whose name was Brian, but who was unaccountably called 'Tim'. He had a strong 'Black Country' accent, and was full of fun and mischief. We shared a love of jazz, and he was a real joy to be with. He was totally blind, like me, and we sometimes stood together when we lined up in the hall for assemblies.

On one occasion when we were in the hall, Mr. S, who was a huge man and a physical education instructor, said to us:

"I don't want another sound out of you."

For some reason Tim laughed. The next sound was that of Mr. S. hurtling towards us, and I felt the wind of his hand as it crashed across Tim's face, knocking him off his feet.

Miss T. was also swift in discipline. She was a masculine sort of woman with a low drawling kind of voice, and she smoked a pipe; and Bob was a boy who 'rocked'. He would sit quietly rocking back and forth in his own world. Psychologists today recognise this as the signs of chronic insecurity, and quite a lot of blind people suffered in this way, but no such excuse was afforded then.

Miss T. made every effort to rid Bob of the habit. Whenever he started to rock, she would drawl sadistically,

"It's coming, Bob," and then she would hurl a book at him. If her aim was good she would hit the defenceless Bob as he tried to protect his head with his arms, but if it was not, then some other unsuspecting child would be struck by the dangerous missile.

No, Kinlet Hall was not a place where one could find understanding and sympathy where most of the staff were concerned, and there were many children who grew up with large 'chips on the shoulder' as a result of this kind of treatment.

In 1943, however, something was to happen which changed the pattern of one whole year for us. It began with a very strange occurrence - we heard an aeroplane approaching.

This was very strange because we were now tucked away in the wilds of Shropshire, miles from any usual flight paths or aerodromes, and we hardly ever heard the sound of planes overhead. So we all listened intently as the sound got nearer and nearer. In fact it got so near that with heart-stopping excitement we knew it had passed right by our window, and had come to rest in a field at the side of the lawn.

We soon discovered that the plane heralded the coming of three thousand American soldiers, who were to camp on one side of our drive. They came for manoeuvres in preparation for what was to be 'D' - Day' - although we did not know that at the time. All we knew was that the Americans had come to help the war effort, and they opened up a whole new life to us.

The long drive up to Kinlet Hall was ideal for their purposes. There were trees and bushes and plenty of room - all ideal for manoeuvres, and they soon established their bivouacs, tents, cookhouse, lorries, Jeeps and other equipment amongst the grounds.

Before long, they were settled in, even to the extent of tarmacking half the drive so that the lorries could pass on it more easily! Then began a time of unprecedented fun and friendship for us, as they responded easily to the presence of fifty or so blind children, and spoilt us on every occasion possible.

They arranged concerts where, of course, we heard them sing 'The Stars and Stripes', and Colonel O'Shea talked to us in class about life in the States. We were open-mouthed with astonishment! Sometimes they gave us rides in the Jeeps, and on the three going-home days of the year, they gave us kit-bags for all our belongings instead of the usual cases, and took us down to the road in a lorry! We would have had to walk the mile-long drive with all our luggage otherwise.

And they gave us candy. This was particularly wonderful to children who had very few sweets in the first place, even less because of the war, and in the second place we were always hungry. We would accept gratefully any kind of extra food, but candy was an unimaginable treat!

A few special friendships were made - two of the soldiers, Ray Miller and Rusty Hendron, built up a particular rapport with some of the lads, and would be remembered ever afterwards. Most of us were eager to make friends because we so lacked friendship in the bleak school surroundings.

It was a great time, but it ended all too soon for us with the coming of 'D' - Day' in 1944. As quickly as they had come, they mysteriously disappeared, and we were left with a void which would probably never be filled at Kinlet.

At last the war was going right. Hitler was almost killed by a bomb, and it looked as though the end was not far off. Perhaps things could begin to get back to normal again.

For us, it meant a move back to the suburbs of Birmingham. We were to go to a place called 'Lickey Grange' between Bromsgrove and Birmingham, which had been owned by Lord Austin of the Austin Motor Company. A plaque was placed on a marble table in the hall saying 'The gift of Lord Austin to the Birmingham Royal Institute to the Blind'.

The move meant a return to civilisation in the minds of most of us, but for me, personally, it was a welcome move nearer home. However, it was to be rather more momentous than that, for not only did we move on my thirteenth birthday, giving me a sense of a new beginning, but on our arrival we discovered that the school had suddenly become co-educational. We were to work alongside girls!

To boys who had not had close contact with girls since kindergarten days, the news was mind-blowing! We had a completely blinkered view of girls - they were like angels to us - creatures who could do no wrong! We had no idea how to speak to them, and how to behave in their company. Many of us became quite inhibited by their presence.

It was some time before boy-girl friendships evolved, but inevitably they did. Eventually the talk was predictable: 'I've got a girl-friend', or 'I'm going out with someone' and 'so am I' they would say.

It was not long before I joined the ranks of the enlightened teenager and acquired myself a girl-friend too. She was a girl I had known at Wolverley, and was very small. In fact, she was so small that when we played 'Hide and Seek', she could hide in a desk! I thought she was wonderful, and had a terrific crush on her!

In general, it was a great year. We were growing up and beginning to think for ourselves, and take more of an interest in the outside world. The war was coming to an end, and people were beginning to look with more hope to the future, and at thirteen, I could now have 'privileges'.

I could go out alone to Bromsgrove which was within walking distance, and enjoy the bustle of the shops. I would wander around Woolworths, and the 'Messenger' newsagents, but I particularly enjoyed the radio shop. It was here that I could buy crystals, headphones and coils with which I could construct my own 'crystal set' radios.

Making crystal sets became a craze which was to last with me for a long time. They were made by assembling a coil of wire, a crystal diode, a condenser and a pair of headphones on to a base. The device was earthed at one end of the wire by attaching it to a radiator or a pipe, then the wire would form the coil and go on to the condenser, continuing through the crystal diode to headphones and an aerial. With this little set, which could be carefully assembled by any reasonably adept youngster, was heard some of the best radio broadcasts of the day, and we found it fascinating.

We made all kinds of crystal sets, but we particularly enjoyed seeing who could make the smallest. I made one from a cotton-reel which was very efficient. We were very near the transmitter at Droitwich that beamed the European Service of the BBC across the continent, so by earthing the set to a radiator and the aerial to the bedspring, we could hear the European Service loud and clear! Many happy hours were spent with these sets, and they were also useful for listening in bed!

Near us in the village of Catshill, was a Methodist Church where we got to know the young people. One of these was a young man who rejoiced in the name of Grenville Wagstaff, and he, too, had a crystal set. However, to my amazement, he had improved it by feeding it through an amplifier. This was a dream! The quality of sound was vastly different and superbly clear. I added the information to my knowledge, and determined that I would improve my sets in the same way as soon as I could.

In 1944 my brother Harry was 'called up' into the Army. He had been a reservist, but he now went on to serve in Northern Ireland, Egypt, Suez and Port Said. He had got married just before he went away, and in 1945 I became an uncle for the first time! My nephew was also called Harry after his father as was the custom, but to avoid confusion, he was known as 'Al'. He grew up to be rather musical himself, becoming a member of a pop-group which achieved some notoriety as the 'Applejacks'.

We were encouraged to write letters at school, and I duly set out to write to my brother who was at that time in Egypt. it was a long time before he got the letter, and when he did, it was covered all over by the stamps of 'British Intelligence'. I had written the letter in Braille, of course, and it had been translated into ordinary writing by a teacher. 'Intelligence', however, did not apparently have this included in their briefing, for they had immediately assumed that the letter was in code - and had tried to decipher it!

It had gone from one department to another, being repeatedly stamped, until finally someone realised that it was genuine Braille and contained nothing sinister! The envelope was kept by the family for years, although the uninteresting letter within, was lost!

There were no further opportunities for British Intelligence to be confused, for in May 1945 the war ended in Europe. 'VE' day was a holiday which we celebrated by going out to the 'Ten-Acre' field nearby and enjoying picnics and games. Even a threatened thunder storm could not dampen our spirits as we rejoiced in the heady atmosphere of the day.

The war finally ended completely in August, and this too, was a day of national rejoicing, the like of which would not be seen for many years. Parties were arranged in the streeets, and my part was to play the piano which was trundled outside to back up the singing.

All this went towards making the year I spent at Lickey one of the most enjoyable of my school days. Perhaps the best part was that Joe and I could go to my house quite often. We would make the journey from the tram terminus at Rednal to Northfield, then change on to a bus which took us near home into King's Heath. One more short bus journey, and we were there.

We enjoyed seeing Mum and Dad and being in home surroundings, but even more importantly, we had food! There was scarcely time for more, because we had to begin the journey back again, but it was worth it!

When we got back to the tram terminus we had to walk back up Rose Hill which was a fairly steep incline. We would arrive at Lickey almost on the point of exhaustion, having delayed so long at home that we were in danger of being reprimanded for being late. In the event, we were never actually cautioned at all, which was an indication of the more laid back, relaxed atmosphere of Lickey.

There was to be one final move in my school years, to the senior school at Carpenter Road, Edgbaston.

Chapter 8

ILLNESS AND OPPORTUNITIES

Carpenter Road was the senior school, taking the fourteen to sixteen year olds. It was still a relaxed atmosphere where we could have a reasonable amount of freedom, and here we came across Mr. Myers who had been a teacher at Bockleton Court. He was the senior teacher now, and since he had political leanings, he made attempts to bring democracy to the school organisation by setting up a school council to include staff and children.

It was a good try, but not altogether successful - perhaps because we had been 'institutionalised' too long, perhaps because we were enjoying a greater freedom now - whatever the reason, we did not fall into Mr. Myers plans too well, and he eventually left.

In a biography of Mr. Myers, 'And You A Gentleman', by Cambray Jones, he explains that Mr. Myers was completely 'out of step' with the ethos of our school. He did not agree with the harshness of our treatment, or with corporal punishment. It tells how he hated the dreaded outdoor inspections which he considered were degrading and unnecessary. Apparently on one occasion he was told to cane a boy, but instead, he beat a cushion and told the boy to scream! He then warned the boy not to offend again, or he would be forced to cane him properly!

Mr. Myers went on to pioneer a school at Condover Hall,

near Shrewsbury, for blind children who had additional handicaps. Later he become an executive with UNESCO[1]

My friend, Joe, also left - or rather went on to another school to finish his education - because he had 'too much sight'. We assured each other that we would keep in touch.

Carpenter Road, however, was nicely available for an immensely exciting event. Two miles away from the school were the BBC's main broadcasting studios in Broad Street, and some of the children and staff were asked to take part in a programme which was part of a series called 'The Future's Here'.

The programme was a mixture of all kinds of things, but it had a dance band to provide the music. I had never before been in the actual presence of a dance band and I was agog with exhilaration. I had heard Alan Airs and his band on the radio many times, but to be here with them was ecstatic! But even more - Harry Engleman was the pianist. I had heard him many times too, but I could hardly believe it when I was given the opportunity to play the piano with him! We played as a duet on one piano, he playing the bass and I playing the top part. It was quite wonderful! Here I was playing on the other side of the radio! Listening on my crystal set would never be the same again!

Another section of the programme was an interview with a man called Bill Bowes. At first I only registered how big his hands were as he shook my hand at the start, but when he began to speak I realised that he was the famous Yorkshire cricketer!

When our turn came, we were announced by Alan Howland, who had been a newsreader. I had to explain how blind people play chess with a board with white sunken squares which had holes for the pieces to fit in. I told how the black pieces were plain, but that the white ones had a point at the top.

But that was not the end of my contribution. I could also perform quite skillfully on the 'bones'. These were two pieces of bone -which were held in one hand and separated by the fingers. Then as the hand was shaken, the bones would click and

---

1 United Nations Educational, Scientific and Cultural Organisation.

tap out a lively rhythm. If you were good at it, then the rhythm could be very lively indeed, and loud too. My friend, Ken, provided the melody on the mouth organ, and together we had a wonderful time!

And so the programme was recorded, and transmitted in the following October.

Soon after the broadcast I was taken ill again. I developed rheumatic pains in my right knee and back which almost completely immobilised me, and when my mother came to see me in the sick bay, she was furious! My pain was so acute that I could not even bear the movement of the bedclothes, and she wanted to know why I had not yet seen a doctor.

She harangued the mild-mannered Mr. Williams who wilted under the onslaught, and then she took me away from the school, insisting that she went with me to hospital.

Very soon a doctor came to see me. After a brief examination, the first thing he said was:

"This young man is suffering from malnutrition."

I was incredibly thin, and the hunger of many years had restricted my physical development. Then he diagnosed a peculiar heart condition which required rest.

With another prolonged stay in hospital, my first thought was to get myself organised with my crystal set. Headphones to the main radio which breadcast throughout the hospital were provided, but I wanted my latest creation.

It was brought in to me, and I earthed it to the radiator which proved fantastic because it was, of course, linked to all the other radiators in the hospital. However, the signal was not really good enough because the hospital was in a built up area. What I needed was a good aerial.

Amazingly, the hospital moved into action. An engineer appeared who rigged up a superb aerial which went right along the ward and out through the window! I could hardly believe how kind they were to me. The result was marvellous!

I had made the set in such a way that I I could get the Home

Service, the Light Programme and other stations, and the reception was now absolutely clear.

When the doctor (whom I suspect had organised it all), came to see me next, he asked:

"How is the crystal set?" I told him:

'Wonderful! Listen to this....." and I handed him the headphones.

"Marvellous!" he agreed."It doesn't shout at you, does it?"

And so I willingly rested, with my ears to the outside world, and took my medicine - which was the most revolting I have ever tasted!

I was glad to be able to go home at Christmas, but I was warned that I must not do anything. I must have complete rest and not get excited.

This was extremely difficult for me, especially when I was home with the family, and at Christmas - the time I loved more than any other. I managed well until after the celebrations, when there was a heavy snowfall.

The snow was inches deep, and my brother and sisters rushed outside. I remained indoors, desperately wishing that I could join in the fun and laughter.

Soon, my sister, Betty, ran in to tell me what was going on.

"We're making a really big snowball!" she cried, 'we're rolling it and making it bigger and bigger - you should come and see it!"

This was just too much. I simply had to go and look.

It was amazing fun. The snowball was getting so big that everyone had to get behind it to push. I couldn't resist it and went to help. The snowball got bigger and we pushed with all our might.

Suddenly I collapsed. They tried to lift me, but it was no good. I had to be carried indoors, and the doctor was called. He confirmed that I had done too much, and that I would now have to rest completely in bed for a few days.

Resting did not prove to be the end of it, however. When I was finally allowed up, I discovered that I was very unsteady on my feet. I would fall over for no apparent reason, and when I had a cup of tea, I could not keep my hand still enough to hold it. So back to hospital I went, and this time was diagnosed as having a mild form of 'St. Vitas' Dance', the remedy for which was almost total immobilisation. I eventually went back to Carpenter Road in March after five months' absence - just in time for the Easter holidays!

On my return to school, I had to face the fact that my illness had come at a very inconvenient time. During our fourteenth year, a choice had to be made which would shape the future.

We were given the option as to whether we would go on to the training workshops, where we would learn upholstery, basketwork and other crafts, or go to the Royal Normal College (later re-named 'Royal National College') which trained piano technicians, tuners and shorthand typists.

I had intended to opt for the Royal Normal College as my interests lay only in working with and playing pianos.

With sadness I realised that I had missed my opportunity. While I had been away ill, the choices had been offered and made, and I had missed the time. Now I would simply have to go to the training college to do upholstery, and I hated the idea. And so began my training in making mattresses.

I did not try very hard. I couldn't concentrate on the work. My thoughts were all at the other college where the lucky students were learning what I had always wanted to do - and here was I struggling with mattresses!

The tutors tried to help. I went from mattresses to basketry, but to no avail. I just couldn't get the hang of it somehow. They tried me on various other crafts too, but my heart was not in any of them. I could not rid myself of the feeling of being cheated out of my true vocation.

It just wasn't fair! To be denied what should have been my choice, simply because I was ill. How could I possibly stick with craft work for the rest of my life?

The boredom of the weeks were punctuated by visits from Joe, and weekends at home. I could at leat play the piano there. I would spend hours lost in the world of jazz and popular music, trying to emulate the musicians of the day. One of those I particularly admired was 'Fats' Waller. He was a rebel, like me.

I knew the story of how he had horrified his minister father by playing jazz on their church organ. 'Fats' was thrown out and told never to come back. He didn't.

I too, was sick of being 'pushed around'. I had been told what to do by other people all my life. I wanted to break out and do what I wanted to do. I wanted to make my own choices, and go my own way. I was fed up with having to comply with what others thought was right for me.

As I threw myself into imitating 'Fats' Waller, there was a knock on the door. I took no notice as the man from the Prudential came in, and my mother gave him the weekly payment. But he didn't rush away. He waited until I had finished what I was playing and then said:

"That was terrific! We've got a twelve piece band and we are playing at Cateswell House Ballroom tomorrow night. Would you come?"

I was overjoyed. This was more like it. At last I would be able to entertain the public. My playing would have a real purpose.

We were given a spot during the evening when the band had gone off. 'We' being myself and my sister, Betty, who liked to think she was Birmingham's answer to Vera Lynn! She sang a few numbers, and then I played, starting off with some 'boogie-woogie', then on to the jives and 'Fats' Waller numbers. The people loved it! My first exposure to public playing was an unqualified success, and I went on from there confidently.

Soon I was accepting bookings to parties, and since my mum and dad were members of the Working Men's Club, I was asked there.

And so began a time of boring days at the workshops, with glittering weekends playing on the party and club circuit. But the end of a party was not necessarily the end of the evening. We would often arm ourselves with a few bottles and go back to someone's house where the carpet would be rolled up and we would begin again, going on until well into the night. Sleep could be forgotten until Sunday morning, when I would be able to lie in bed until lunchtime and make up a few lost hours. On Monday mornings my world would drastically change as I went back to the dreary upholstery training.

The training centre was in the building which had once been my old school at Harborne. It seemed strange to be there again after so many years. I noticed that things which had been big before, were now small. I had once hardly been able to reach the border round the wall. Now it was at my shoulder level. The swinging wash bowls were still there, but instead of having to reach up to them, we now had to duck over them. It was all so different - and yet the same place.

As I walked up to the workshops from the training centre, my feet dragged and my head drooped. I didn't feel I could cope with day after day of upholstery. If only I could get enough piano playing work - perhaps I could make a living at that instead.

The upholstery teacher was a Mr. Thatcher who had been a supervisor at Carpenter Road. One day he summoned me to a meeting of the committee.

"We have been trying to train you for a job," he began, 'but you don't seem to be interested in anything we offer you. You've tried upholstery, bedding and basketry. What are you going to do with your life?"

Sadly I answered truthfully, 'I only want to play the piano. I just can't get interested in anything else."

"Yes," answered Mr. Thatcher, patiently. 'I remember your playing when I was supervising. You love the piano and music?"

"It's what I want to do more than anything." I responded.

The committee members looked at one another. Mr. Thatcher continued.

"Well, that's what we have been discussing." He shifted his

position and went on. "We have brought you here to ask you how you would feel about transferring to the Royal Normal College so that you can learn tuning and repairing, and to further your studies in music?"

"But .....but I thought I'd missed the chance to do that," I stammered.

"Yes, but we're giving you another chance as you were ill when the choices were made."

I was ecstatic! It was what I wanted most. I realised that it would curtail my embrionic career as a public musician, but I had enough sense to grasp that it would be only a temporary lull whilst I trained for a profession. I could return to the circuit later.

My cup was quite full when they told me that the training fees would be paid by the local authority, and that if I returned with a piano tuning diploma, then they would guarantee me a job.

The Birmingham City Authority could do no more for me than that. I will always be grateful for their help. They were wonderful!

Chapter 9

A CHANGED LIFE

I was seventeen when I started college in April 1949, and although I was very glad to be there, I had to get used to being under authority once again. Having had a time of relative relaxation, I was now back in what amounted to residential school, and that meant regimentation, rules and regulations. I could no longer get off home for the weekends quite so easily, because the college was fifty miles away between Shrewsbury and Welshpool.

In order to deal with the rules I needed to make friends quickly. They would be able to explain which rules could never be broken, and which could be safely bent! One place where I would be bound to meet friends was at the Saturday night dance. This was - inevitably - a supervised affair, in which pianists were provided sometimes by staff and sometimes by students.

As soon as it was discovered that I was a strict-tempo pianist, I was asked to go on the rota. It was no problem to me to play for the waltzes, foxtrots, quicksteps, tangos, and all the other dances which made up the evening's entertainment, and I willingly agreed.

When I duly turned up for my stint, I was stopped in my tracks by the sound of the pianist who preceded me. He was amazingly good.

"Who's that?" I asked in admiration.

"Oh, that's John - he just a junior," my companion answered scornfully. 'Seniors don't fraternise with juniors."

"This senior does!" I returned quickly, and went straight over to the piano.

"That was marvellous!" I said to him.

Shyly he answered: "Oh, thanks. Do you really like it?"

"It was great!" I assured him genuinely, and cemented the start of our friendship.

One of the things I hated most about institutional living, was the obligatory church attendance. All through my school days church had been incredibly boring and beyond our level of understanding. I had determined that at the first opportunity, I would stop going. I did not include in this opinion, the Sunday Schools which I had attended. They were a different thing altogether. They were aimed at children, and consisted of activities which children liked. 'Church' was not aimed at children - in fact, in my experience, children had been an unwelcome appendage to the rest of the congregation.

But here at college, I could not avoid going. Once more it was obligatory, and it infuriated me. I was not a child any longer, and they had no right to insist that I complied in this way! I was perfectly willing to comply when it came to the training - that was necessary, but church attendance was not necessary to my piano tuning course, and I couldn't see why it was insisted upon.

So here we were again, on a bright morning in May, forming the usual 'crocodile' - just like a crowd of little children - and leading off to the weekly dose of boredom. I fumed as I walked along in the line. I didn't need this. Religion was a 'crutch' for the young and the elderly who had got nothing else in life to keep them going. I intended to make my way in show business, and church would not form part of that. I had no intention of submitting to religion simply because it was the 'thing to do'.

As we entered the church, I anticipated the usual musty smell of old pews and worn hassocks. To my surprise, a smell of fresh paint met my critical nose. This church had a strange 'clean' smell to it, and did not have the kind of atmosphere I expected at all. I knew the service would be the same old thing, though,

84

and I continued to fume as we stood, sat and knelt in the appropriate places.

As the sermon droned on, I fidgeted and scowled until twenty interminable minutes later, the vicar stopped, and we prepared to stand for the last hymn. We didn't hear the introduction to it for the tearing, ripping sound which met our ears. The pews had been newly varnished a few days before, and the warm morning and long sermon had ensured that we stuck firmly to the tacky seats! The rest of the students fell about with laughter, but I did not find it funny. To me it was a symbol of the 'holding' power of religion to the masses. I was not only forced to attend - it seemed as though they were even trying to keep me there!

The only disappointing thing about my friendship with John was the fact that he attended the college Christian Fellowship. He asked me to go too, but of course, I did not want anything to do with it. I had better things to do with my time.

At home I had used Sunday as a 'recovery' day. On Saturday nights I would play at Catewell House at the dinners in the officers' mess where the officers brought their wives or girl-friends - sometimes both! They used to play 'Housey-Housey', (which is 'Bingo' in today's 'Revised Standard Version'!) then have dinner, during which time I would play gently; then they would give me a fee, call me a taxi, and send me home. Since I liked to have my full eight hours of sleep, I would therefore spend all Sunday morning catching up with them.

I had been a free agent then. Now here I was, back under authority, having to submit to prayers every day and church on Sunday morning, and John was asking if I would go to the Christian Fellowship on Sunday afternoons!

"The great thing about it is that there are no staff there!" urged John, who knew where to hit me hardest.

"I'm interested, then," I answered. If it was the only place where I could avoid the endless supervision, then that would have to be the place to be. Only one more thing was necessary.

"Do you play the piano there?" I asked.

"Yes," he confirmed, "we have a rota, I take my turn."

"Okay then," I told him, "next time you are playing, I'll come." I really enjoyed hearing him play.

"Good!" he replied, "because actually, I'm playing next Sunday!"

It seemed like a continuing conspiracy to get me involved in religion! I didn't seem to be able to get a break from it at all! I had to be as good as my word, and so I duly went off to the next meeting. There was only a small group of students, and what they sang and said seemed vaguely familiar to me. Some of the songs they sang were like those I had learned as a small child, and when they prayed it sounded just as Miss Richardson had prayed - like talking to someone real - a personal friend or a loving father. It was not a bit like the pompous religiosity I had experienced in church. It was like a step back into the past. Nostalgia swept over me, and I remembered the time as a young child when I had asked Jesus to come into my life.

Then someone read from Psalm 139. The psalmist was saying "Lord, you know when I go to bed, when I get up, when I sit down and when I stand up. You know what I think before I think it, what I'm going to say before I say it. You're in front of me, behind me, and your hand is on top of me. I can't cope with that knowledge - it's too wonderful for me. I tried to get away from you but I can't. I've tried distance, but everywhere is near to you. I've tried darkness, but everywhere is light to you. So Lord, I just give up. I want you to search me, try me, and lead me in the way everlasting."

This really spoke to me. I didn't intend that it should - for one thing I didn't like Psalms. They were always badly chanted in church, and this offended my musical ear; but in school Psalms had been synonymous with punishment. If you misbehaved in church, you had to write out a psalm.

But this psalm spoke to me in spite of myself. It told me that I could not avoid God. I couldn't hide from someone who is everywhere.

So I continued to go to the Christian Fellowship, taking my turn at playing the piano by the end of the term. I was not going to make any kind of commitment, but simply keep my options open.

When I went home for the summer holidays, I was able to tell the family that my tuning had gone well. It seemed as though I was born for it. I had already taken two tests, and was therefore well ahead of the usual time-scale for the course.

My keenness, however, did not impress the local lads who came round for a band session. I was no longer very interested in this kind of thing, and they turned away scornfully.

"One term at college," they said, "and he's a snob already!"

It wasn't that, though. My appetites and ambitions were changing subtly. My life was beginning to go in a different direction and I was maturing fast.

It was my sister, Betty, who instigated the visit to Birmingham Town Hall to hear the American evangelists. She came excitedly home one day with the news that a boy preacher was to speak at the town hall in a series of meetings, and she talked me into going to hear him with her.

The main attraction was to be David Walker, a young boy with an unmistakable charisma. The Americans, perhaps unwisely, made much of child evangelists in those days, and 'Little David' toured with the team, telling about his amazing experiences with God.

I went with Betty on the Friday night. We had never been in such a huge meeting before - there were over two thousand people there, all singing rousing hymns complete with descants! The atmosphere was electric! This was nothing like the religious meetings I had ever been to before. It was not in the least dull or boring. It was vibrant and meaningful, and seemed to bring God right down to us, rather than being a remote entity somewhere in the clouds.

We went again on the Saturday night, and by this time I was coming to a crisis point. All I had heard and seen over recent months was going round and round in my mind, and I felt compelled to go on until I reached some kind of conclusion. I sensed that I was on the verge of something enormous, but I could not quite grasp it. The exciting meeting fired me a little further, and on the Sunday I decided to go to the chapel where I had attended Sunday School.

I had not been forgotten there. I was welcomed with open arms and a great deal of adulation! I began to feel as though I belonged.

There was to be an afternoon meeting at the Town Hall, beginning at three o'clock. I was determined to go, although it meant forgoing dinner. Dad had a standing arrangement at the 'Dog and Partridge' on Sundays until 2.30pm, so lunch was put off until he came home. I could not wait that long, so went straight on to the Town Hall without it.

I listened enrapt as 'Little David' told his story. It was an extraordinary story.

He had always been something of a 'mystical' child, going often into the woods to pray. One afternoon when he was only seven years old, he was in his bedroom praying when he felt himself being lifted. Suddenly he found himself walking through fields by a river. He could see fruit trees - beautiful trees - he had never seen anything so beautiful, and he had never seen a river so clear - it was as clear as crystal. There was a city in the distance, clothed with light. He took in the glorious scene, noticing that there did not seem to be any weather. There did not even seem to be any sunshine, yet a soft, beautiful and wonderful light pervaded everything.

Then he was aware of someone coming towards him in a kind of cloud. He didn't want to go back, so he began to cry. The figure spoke to him from the cloud, saying that he was going back to earth to tell people about the river and the city. He was to tell them about the peace, the joy and the happiness, and about the place where Jesus wanted them to be.

He knew then that he was speaking with Jesus himself. There

was something beautiful and calming about the voice, and yet Little David cried because he didn't want to go back. Jesus told him 'you must go, but you will come back again'.

When he found himself back in his room, it was seven o'clock in the evening, and he had been praying for five hours.

There were no doubts in my mind that what 'Little David' had described was true. The importance of his experience seemed to reach right into my soul and fitted together with all the other experiences I had had recently into some kind of pattern. There was no doubt that Jesus Christ was challenging me to place my life and my whole future in his hands.

I had had nothing but an orange to eat that day, and yet when I got home I told the family that I was going to my room; I did not want any tea and I did not want to be disturbed.

I thought over what I had heard. I did not expect to be 'lifted' like Little David - that was a 'one-off' experience for people who came from America to tell people like me that heaven was real - but I was conscious of a sadness. I became aware that even as a child growing into a young man, I had let Jesus down. Seven years before, I had received him as a Saviour and had taken him at his word, but I had not continued with him.

Could I ever sustain such a commitment? I had no doubts about Jesus' faithfulness to me - it was my faithfulness to him which worried me. Would I be able to withstand the pressures of college life? I had messed it up at school when instead of being spiritual I became physical, and now the pressures would be much more academic, intellectual, scientific and perhaps philosophical. Would I fail with Jesus again? I didn't want to put my hand to the plough unless I knew I wouldn't look back.

For some time I was obsessed with this difficult problem. Then suddenly it came to me that Jesus didn't die for people who would be successful - he died for failures. The cross was the price he paid, whether I failed or succeeded - there could be no change in that. There was no altering the fact that Jesus died for me whether I failed or succeeded. So to refuse what he had done for me would be the biggest failure of all!

That was the end of the line. I had no further arguments. I just 'caved in' and submitted to the Lord Jesus. As I sat there alone in my room, I prayed: 'Lord, whether I fail or succeed, I want to belong to you - that's all that matters'. Verses I had learned as a child came back to me.

'He that comes to me I will in no wise cast out'; 'Behold I stand at the door and knock, if anyone hears my voice and opens the door, I will come in and sup with him and he with me'. 'I am the door, by me if any man enter in, he shall be saved'.

I know now that these were Scriptures of accessibility - Jesus giving me access and I giving Jesus access. The gospel was mutual - I possess him, but he possesses me. We possess each other. This was a relationship which was being born on me by the Holy Spirit. I was being called into relationship. I understood that Jesus had won the victory on Calvary, so I was restored!

Years later, this experience was to formulate in messages I would bring to young people who perhaps, like me, made a commitment in childhood, but who fell away and then counted it for nothing. It is never 'nothing' - it is a foundation which God will work on in time.

I recognised the joy of being restored. From God's side, the relationship had not been broken, it was only broken from my side. He had held his end of the bond, and was waiting for me to take up my end.

Later that evening I went to the Youth Club where I played for the service. Afterwards we had refreshments, during which time I would usually play requests of all the popular music of the day. Soon someone asked me to play, and they gathered around the piano as I began to play 'Twelfth Street Rag'.

Suddenly it all felt out of place. I had to stop and explain.

"I've had a wonderful experience with Jesus," I began. "I just can't play that kind of music any more. I am now in love with Jesus, and everything else seems unimportant."

Being 'in love' was the only way I could describe what had

happened. I had been in love in a youthful fashion with Rene, a girl at school, and the experience I was now going through was as emotional as that. It came up from deep inside me together with a feeling of gratitude and awareness. It was tremendous!

They didn't understand, of course, but it marked the first time I had witnessed to someone of my new faith.

The folk at the Christian Fellowship at college were delighted, however. I was obviously convinced, and had had an experience which no-one could talk me out of - although plenty of the students tried! I told as many as possible about Jesus, expecting that as soon as they knew, they too, would believe and be saved. I couldn't understand why they didn't! I didn't know why the same experience shouldn't happen to everyone else! There were those who did come to know the Lord, however, and we were able to hold counselling sessions for them to help them on their way.

From that time on, the meetings of the Christian Fellowship had a different emphasis as I poured everything into evangelism. Perhaps I was not too wise, but God beautifully overruled in my enthusiasm.

The one thing that began to puzzle me was how I was to serve God. How could I give him what I had to offer? I longed to play the piano, but Christian music was very staid and plain at the time, with most of the hymns in four-part harmony, and there was no scope for the kind of playing I enjoyed. I prayerfully thought and wondered what God had in store for me.

My college work progressed very well. I learned to tune pianos, advanced my studies in music, and learned to type. They were wonderful, formative years, and probably the most productive of my life. I relaxed in the knowledge that the crisis for me was over. I was now related to God by receiving and accepting Jesus Christ, and I could confidently face the future and whatever it held.

Chapter 10

WINNING FOR GOD

It was good to see my friend, Joe, from time to time. He would make the long journey from Wolverhampton to the college, or sometimes I would meet him in Shrewsbury. He loved pop music, and I would play for him, although I was no longer quite so keen on this kind of music.

On one of his visits, he brought me a little battery driven radio. I thanked him, but had no idea what it was going to mean to me. I took it to bed with me, and as usual, explored through the wavebands for a while before going to sleep. Suddenly I heard the sound of amazing piano playing. But it was not just the playing - it was what was played that attracted my attention. It was a gospel chorus: 'Heavenly sunshine, heavenly sunshine, flooding my soul with glory divine!' and there was no formal four-part harmony here - it was brilliant, lively music, from a pianist who was obviously not inhibited in his playing at all! Then the cheerful voice of Charles E. Fuller urged the listeners to sing along, then turn around and shake hands with a neighbour and enjoy the 'Heavenly sunshine of the Lord!'

I no longer wanted to go to sleep, and although I was in no position to comply with Mr. Fuller's request, I listened with rapt attention as Rudi Attwood drew wonderful sounds from his piano. There I was in bed, but catapulted in my memory to the Town Hall, Birmingham, where I had heard gospel playing for the first time, and where my experience with the Lord had begun.

I couldn't stay in the dormitory with the others to hear this, they had no interest in the gospel, so I got out of bed and went down the corridor to the washroom and closed the door behind me. Down the right side of the bathroom was a line of hand basins and a wide window sill. I counted three basins to the window, climbed up onto the sill, turned on the hot water tap and put my feet into the warm water. In this way, from that night, every Thursday I would remain warm enough to sit and listen to 'The Old Fashioned Revival Hour' on Radio Luxembourg, and the phenomenal pianist who accompanied the singing!

It must be said that I got a blessing every Thursday night in number three wash-basin; and on Friday morning I had the cleanest pair of feet in the college! I regret that I never made a contribution to the listener's letters section of the programme. For I fancy that if Mrs. Fuller (whom Charles called 'Honey') had received a letter from me she would have loved saying: 'Now we have a letter from a young man who listens to our programme in a bathroom with his feet in a hand basin of hot water to keep warm! It would have brought the house down in the studios in Long beach, California!

One night as I listened to Rudi Attwood's masterful playing, I prayed:

"Lord, if I can play even half as well as Rudi Attwood, I will be a gospel pianist for you one day." God answered that prayer - I am just about half as good as Rudi Attwood! I should have prayed : '.....if I can be *as good* as him....' - I might have been twice the pianist I am!

Throughout my remaining time at college, my willingness to speak about the Lord to anyone who would listen - and some who wouldn't - earned me the nickname of 'Father Jackson', amongst others, but at least they all knew that I was a Christian and what I stood for.

Joe and I had known each other a good many years by now, and he had proved himself to be a very faithful friend. His visits to me were no small sacrifice, travelling quite long distances so that we would keep in touch.

He, therefore, became on of my chief concerns, now that I had discovered the truth of the Gospel. Joe had been brought up as a Roman Catholic, and although he still kept a thin contact with his priest, there was not much more to it than that. I wanted him to have the same vibrant faith as I had found, and I prayed for him often.

I was particularly burdened one weekend when Joe was to visit me again on the Saturday. I determined to spend some time in prayer on his behalf before he arrived. So on the Friday evening I took myself into one of the practice rooms which could not be used for practice after eight o'clock, and set myself to pray for Joe.

As a new, enthusiastic Christian, I became very emotional when something touched me deeply, and I felt a desperation for Joe which drove me into fervent prayer. I told myself that I should not get so 'het up' over it all, and that perhaps I had gone a little 'over the top' in my efforts. I tried to calm myself down.

I met Joe in Shrewsbury the next day, and we went off the 'Prince Rupert Cafe' for a bite to eat. We finished our egg and chips and went off to the area of parkland known locally as 'The Quarry', and sat down for a while. I handed Joe a small tract which said 'For God so loved the world that he gave his only begotten son that whosoever believeth in him shall not perish but shall have everlasting life'. But where the word 'whosoever' should have been was a blank space where one could add one's own name instead.

I said: "Do read his, Joe, and see if you can put your name in the blank space."

We eventually strolled off in the direction of the bus stop, but as we went, we passed an open air Salvation Army meeting going on. Suddenly, to my amazement, I heard my name called and the officer saying,

"Come and give us a word, brother!"

It was a total surprise to me, but as it happened, that week I had seen a lovely text at the end of the first book of Samuel, chapter nine. It said '.....stay here awhile, so that I may give you a message from God.' What better text could you have for an open air message? It actually asks the people going by to stay and listen! I jumped up on to the rostrum and preached, and when I had finished, we hurried off to the bus. Joe and I shook hands and we parted.

By the middle of the next week, I had a letter from Joe which said, 'I listened to what you said, I read the tract, and I have filled in my name. Then I went to the priest and said 'with great respect, I've no longer any need for your services because I have found Jesus as my Saviour',

I cannot explain how much that meant to me. It encouraged me like nothing else could have done.

Throughout my college years, however, I was to come under influences which were to challenge my young, but developing faith. There were times when I had to re-assess what I had learned, but instead of shaking my faith, it served to strengthen and consolidate it.

One of these influences came from a Mr. Sanderson, whom I met through the girl who lived next door to us at home. She was a Christadelphian, and was keen for me to become one, too. Mr. Sanderson went to her meeting, and she introduced me to him one day. He was a travelling salesman who sold ladies fashion hats, and his work sometimes brought him to Shrewsbury. When he could, he would visit me and talk about the Christadelphian way.

He was a very nice man whose generosity and kindness impressed me greatly. He told me various things which conflicted with what I thought I knew of Christianity. He said that Christadelphians do not believe in a personal devil, and that evil is simply thoughts and inclinations. He explained that the Bible's description of Jesus facing Satan in the wilderness was imagery, with Jesus possessing the normal thoughts which had to be fought and worked out for himself.

I did not dismiss all that I was told, but I had to make some kind of assessment of what these very kind people were saying, and try to find out where the truth really lay.

First of all, I went to my pastor, and discussed with him what I had heard. We spent some time looking at the Scriptures, and he tried to show me what the Bible said. I looked into it very carefully, studying what was written about the origins of evil, and I came to the conclusion that it could not possibly be a vague influence - it had to be a power. And just as there was the person of the Godhead, I saw that evil was manifested in the form of a person. I also read the book 'Mere Christianity' by C.S. Lewis, and gained better understanding through his explanation of 'dualism'.

I also had to find out the truth about the Holy Spirit of God. Again they said that this was just the power of God, or his influence, and I felt I must look at this very carefully. When I came across the verse in Ephesians chapter four where it says 'grieve not the Holy Spirit of God', I wondered how one could grieve a power or an influence. 'Grieve' is a word of emotion, and only possible in a person. I just could not believe the Christadelphian idea, and my researches were serving to strengthen my faith.

I found the arguments of the Seventh Day Adventists more convincing. I was receiving a magazine from America which was very good, but often had articles about the Sabbath being on the seventh day instead of the first day of the week, and their arguments were very powerful.

I used to go to some of their meetings and I found them more of a challenge in a way, because this argument had more credence - especially when I read the Old Testament which said over and over again 'this shall be a Sabbath unto you for ever and ever'.

I found I had more in common with the Seventh Day Adventists who did believe in the deity of Christ, and in his sacrifice for sin, but I had difficulty with their legalism in other areas. All this, too, I discussed with my pastor.

The greatest challenge came, however, from another direction. As our Evangelicalism grew throughout the college, a counter-culture developed, and this proved to be far more sinister.

There was a young man at college who had mediumistic qualities, and he formed a 'circle'. These people did not come to our Christian Fellowship, of course, and they seemed concerned that I should become part of their circle. So they invited me to one of their meetings.

I had read nothing about spiritualism, and had absolutely no idea as to what to expect; but I had read something in 1John chapter four which said 'test the spirits to see whether they are from God'. These young people used that reference to point out that the spirits 'come through and talk to us'.

I was fascinated and went along to the circle meeting.

Bernard, the medium could fall into a trance almost at will, during which time his normal rhythmic breathing gave way to long drawn-out breaths. It was eerie - he did not seem to draw normal breaths at all, it was just long, long, breathing. I sat there, enthraled.

Sure enough, before long, a voice began to speak - but it was not Bernard's voice although it came from his mouth. It was asked questions, and at one point I was welcomed into the circle. I sat amazed as I was then told that if I continued in my zeal by attending the meetings, I would get wonderful revelations from the spirit world and the Astral plane.

I could hardly believe it! It was obviously for real and the voice was addressing me! This was really something! Of course I would attend the meetings - I wanted to hear more! I was a young Christian, and very keen to learn but my keenness made me very vulnerable.

There was only one problem which niggled in my mind. I knew that the Bible said that there was only one mediator between God and man, and that was Jesus. But all the voices which we heard seemed to be trying to mediate too. I would need to find out what it all meant.

When the holidays arrived I went hot-foot to my pastor. I was overflowing with the wonderful revelation and the 'outworking of faith' - as I saw it. He did not condemn anything I had told him, but quietly responded:

"Right. Let's see what the Bible says about it - as we usually do."

That was fine by me. I had nothing to fear by looking at the Scriptures. So I went round to his house, and we sat down to see what we could discover from the Bible. I soon discovered that God was against all mediumistic practices, and communicating with the dead.

Any manifestations of this kind were forbidden, together with crystal ball gazing. From time to time God gave prophecies, but these were not meant to be peeps into the future, they were given for specific reasons as signposts along the way. In fact, the pastor showed me scriptures that talked about wizards that 'peeped and muttered'.

I came away firmly convinced that Spiritualism is not only wrong but dangerous, and I thank God that in my keenness and profound respect for the Pastor, I saw the truth of what he was teaching me.

When I went back to college, I told the people in the circle that I wanted nothing more to do with them, because their practices were against what God has said. The voices they heard were challenging the mediatorship of Christ and devaluing him, even to the point of trying to de-throne him! I could not go along with anything like that, and I spent the remainder of my time at college militating against the circle.

The matter came to a spectacular head - significantly enough, on Hallowe'en.

The circle, which included well-meaning and sincere people who claimed that they were on the side of the forces of light, met to combat the force of evil which on this night is traditionally dominant. Their meeting took place in the organ practice room, which was larger than the other rooms, and gave them more space. I decided that I would pray in the practice room next door. And so I settled down to pray urgently against what was going on in the next room.

A while later, there was a knock on the door. It opened, and someone said,

"Who is there?"

"Me," I answered, and added "I want you to know that I'm praying against you and I'm asking God that he will destroy this circle."

"Ah, I thought so." responded the voice, "We were told by one of the spirits that there was someone evil next door."

"Be careful," I warned, "because you are on dangerous ground."

About fifteen minutes later the door burst open. There was no knock this time, just a person in desperate panic.

"Please come and help us," the voice pleaded, "the spirits are threatening that they will either send Bernard back to us mad, or else they will kill him......!"

Quickly I followed him into their room, and in the centre of the circle I quoted from Romans chapter eight:

"If God be for us, who can be against us?" and then 1 Corinthians chapter 15, verse 57:

"Thanks be to God who giveth us the victory in our Lord Jesus Christ." Then I said to Bernard, "In the name of Jesus Christ who was manifested to destroy the works of the devil, I command that you come back."

Strange noises came from Bernard as he came out of the deep, deep trance, and as he became conscious, he asked for a glass of water. We gave it to him, and I prayed a prayer of thanksgiving. I also prayed that God would cleanse the place of wickedness.

When he had recovered, Bernard told us that he had experienced being in a temple-like area, (which, as he was partially-sighted, he would understand what it looked like) and that all around there were beings dancing and getting closer and closer to him. He knew they were evil and felt very threatened and frightened. Suddenly he saw a soldier coming towards him. He recognised him as a soldier because he carried a sword, but it had fire all around it.

The soldier simply 'mowed through' the evil, dancing hordes with his burning sword, and they evaporated away. Then he found himself back in the practice room.

I needed no more to convince me of the danger of the occult and of the importance of the teaching of the Bible, especially when it says in Ephesians chapter six, that we must take on 'the whole armour of God'. This was not figurative language in the spirit would - it was literal!

But that was not entirely the end of the matter. In view of the scare that the episode had caused, I decided to take some very practical action. I went to the principal of the college and reported that a group of students were holding regular seances. As a Methodist with very balanced views of Christian things, the principal was horrified, and made an announcement at assembly. He said that if anyone was found dabbling with the occult, they would be immediately expelled.

The devil had overplayed his hand, and God had won a decisive victory in the lives of gullible young people.

My remaining days at college went by quickly and I got through the tuning course ahead of schedule. The time came when I would take my exams in London at the Northern Polytechnic. Passing with honours meant that I would be presented with my certificate by a guest speaker on Speech Day. I was thrilled to learn that the guest would be none other than the eminent conductor Adrian Boult (later 'Sir' Adrian), and shaking the great man's hand seemed to mean more to me than passing the exam!

After gaining my diploma, I was to spend one more term at college. I could have stayed for at least another year to study degrees in music, piano and organ, but the news from home was not too good.

I had been aware for some time that the health of my father was declining. During the war his work as a gold beater had come to an end, and he had moved on to the metals division of ICI, working in the heat, smoke and molten metal of the casting shop which had played havoc with his health. He was also a heavy smoker, making his own cigarettes when he could not afford to buy any, and all this had taken its toll of his lungs. He coughed profusely, and in winter suffered with pneumonia and pleurisy which caused him great pain.

He was now hardly able to work, and as my brother and sisters were now married, my mother was the only breadwinner. I told them that I would spend one last term at college, then I would take up my responsibility to help with the finances at home.

Before returning to college for the last term, I called in to the training school at Harborne to see Mr. Edkins who was now in charge of job allocations, and a senior member of the Birmingham authority. As it happened, it was my twenty-first birthday, and I told him my plans, asking him if they could provide me with a job when I had finished my studies.

He looked at my diploma and records, and said,

"Well, well, so you are twenty-one today!" He smiled at me across the table, and continued, 'Right. Here is our twenty-first birthday present to you. You can start work on Monday January the third!"

Gratefully, I went back to college secure in the knowledge that I had an income guaranteed. This was no small gift in those days, when the advent of television was causing a sever slump in the piano trade. But before I was to begin my tuning career, I had a whole term ahead of me, I was 'of age', and I had *privileges*.

Chapter 11

A NEW DIRECTION

I started my last term at college in enthusiastic anticipation. Twenty-one was considered the age of responsibility, and a watershed in the life of a young man. So long as college work was attended to, and we were there in time for our studies, we were allowed to go anywhere and do more or less as we liked. There was lots to do and the future was promising.

One of the activities I got involved in at this time was the college accordion band - not to play an accordion, but to accompany them on the piano. I reasoned that God would use all my training, both classical and in Jazz to make me into a gospel pianist, and as I studied the style of Rudi Attwood, I realised that to communicate on the piano it is useful to play by ear and use all kinds of music styles. So partly for my own enjoyment, and partly to help them, I joined the group and went around to their various engagements.

At one such engagement, we realised with some consternation that there was no piano. At first we were non-plussed, then I decided to brazen it out.

"Never mind, chaps," I said cheerfully, "you just play normally, and I'll conduct you, no-one will know any different!"

So we went on with the performance. They played all their usual numbers, and I stood in front waving my arms like a conductor. And no-one realised a thing! We had a good laugh afterwards, and joked that it had brought new emphasis to the phrase 'the blind leading the blind!'

With my new status as an official adult, I was now allowed to stay away from college at weekends if I so wished, and since my girl-friend Rene, lived in Hillmorton, near Rugby, sometimes I did so wish!

A few times, therefore, during that term, I took advantage of the X96 Midland Red bus service which went straight from Shrewsbury to Northampton, stopping at Hillmorton, and booked myself into the 'Red Lion' there.

Rene was registered partially sighted, which meant that she had a little vision, and I had already introduced her to my family, who all seemed to like her. I, in turn, seemed to be accepted by her family, so I was quite determined that we would get engaged that term and then marry in the reasonably near future.

During these weekend visits, I sometimes played the piano for Youth Night gettogethers at the home of Sargent Ramsey Maule of the Shrewsbury police force. He and his wife Muriel, and their two daughters, Joy and Jill, attended the church at Shrewsbury, which my new freedom now allowed me to attend. Sometimes the young people would go back to their home, and I would play while they all sang. Then tea would be brought out, and afterwards I would get back to college late, having had a great time.

Sargent Maule was a big man with a big voice, and a certain amount of character. The story went that he would pop round the corner from the police station to have his hair cut at the barbers, but on finding a long queue, he would ask the barber to give him a call when the queue had gone.

"Certainly, Sargent Maule," he would agree with a twinkle in his eye.

About an hour later, a 999 call would be received at the station, and Sargent Maule would don his cap and go off for his hair-cut!

I was also very pleased at this time to meet up with the Tolleys again. It was nine years since I had seen them, but I had never forgotten their kindness to me when I was so ill. They were overjoyed to learn that I had found a living faith, particularly when they heard that it had all really started with them.

Mrs. Tolley was fully convinced of my conversion after she accompanied me to the bus stop on my way back to college, and watched to see it I would light up a cigarette when I thought I was out of her view! I did not light up, since like her, I could not equate it with being a Christian, and she went away happy.

As I became more and more involved in the young people's work in Shrewsbury, my weekends were taken up with playing for the youth rallies which took place around the area. One of these was the Nurse's Fellowship at the Royal Salop. Infirmary, where I continued to go after I had left college, by which time I had also become the speaker for some occasions.

Rene accompanied me to many of these meetings for which I was increasingly asked to play. She was not entirely happy about the arrangement, feeling rather out of her depth in Christian circles, but she wanted to be with me. I was certain that I was in love with her, and after a meeting one day, I resolved to do something about it.

"I'd dearly like to get engaged," I said, earnestly.

"Yes," she agreed, excitedly, 'that would be wonderful."

We went on to talk about our future plans, but somehow I could not raise the kind of enthusiasm which I felt I ought to have. I sensed a reluctance on Rene's part when I talked about the Christian work I hoped to do in the future, but when she tried to settle the matter by saying,

"Well, when we are married, you could have your friends and I could have mine," I heard alarm bells ringing. For some time I prayed and agonised over the problem. I was so much in love, and yet felt very uneasy about our future together.

Finally and with great reluctance, I had to admit that we would have to part. Rene was, naturally, very upset, and tried to contact me sometimes, but I was very busy with crusades and meetings, and she gave up. A year later she married someone else, and eventually had four sons.

My last college days were exciting and fulfilling, but they came to an end in December. So in January 1953, I began my first job with the Birmingham Workshops, taking on more of the tuning than the repairing of the pianos. I loved it! I enjoyed the work, and meeting the people, and I was really happy. Working in an area which I knew well, soon meant that I came across people who had helped me when I was young, and a whole lot of new friendships blossomed.

One evening on my way home from church, I happened to hear someone talking about the wonderful time they had had at their church. They mentioned the excellent prayer meeting, and talked about the sheer beauty of the presence of God. That was the kind of thing I was looking for, and I made up my mind to start going to that church.

I liked it there so much that soon I became a member, and met up with some lovely people, two of whom were Grace and Reg Thomlinson. I had known Grace's mother when I was young, and it was now good to strike up a friendship with Grace and her husband. They were completely 'sold out for God', and involved in gospel music, singing together as a duet.

They introduced me to the new songs which were flooding the Christian market, and beforelong we found ourselves being booked as a three-some, with me accompanying their singing at 'Youth for Christ' meetings.

The 'Youth for Christ' organisation at Birmingham was very big. Their meetings were so well attended that there were queues to get in! We had a great time at these lively meetings, and I was particularly interested when they held a competition to compose a new song. I was thrilled to discover that I came first! At the next competition I came second, and this succeeded in bringing to the public notice what a young blind man was doing for God. I seemed to be some kind of freak - no other blind people were doing this. It attracted attention, and since I wanted to serve God, it served my purpose - and his - that I should be noticed.

These were wonderful days of evangelism, with a great deal

of input coming from the Americans, who were learning that the technology of the entertainment world could be used for God. The Billy Graham organisation did most to put it into action, and so a series of professionally made evangelical films soon began to be shown throughout the country.

The first we saw at our church was 'Mr. Texas'. Here was a new phenomenon: the Christian message put across in the same manner as the media marketed their products. We were agog at the audacity of the production, and at the immensity of the costs involved. This was working for God in a really big way!

I was awed by the sheer professionalism of the musicians: Ted Smith on the piano, and Paul Mickleson on the organ. But when George Beverley Shea sang 'Just A Closer Walk With Thee', I melted! It was also a lesson to me. Somehow I had become used to the brashness of the pop world, where people were promoted with their songs. Here it was different. There was virtuosity, but with humbleness. The message was the important thing, not the people, and the message was promoted in the best possible way. The results were dynamic. Thousands of people were reached and lives were changed. This was the age of top line evangelism.

The theme was picked up by other organisations as their finances would allow, and the National Young Life Campaign was one of these. They launched crusades everywhere, and Grace, Reg and I were invited to take part. We also undertook church-based campaigns on our own, working with speakers such as Don Summers, Frank Farley, Marshall Shallis and Roy Hession.

In order to give us a greater freedom of travel, Grace and Reg bought a large caravan, and I set aside my tuning work for the time being, to travel around with them, living in a small room at one end of the caravan. It was cramped and not very convenient, but I didn't mind. I was doing what I wanted to do above all else.

Spreading the Gospel was more important than anything, and we appreciated the privilege of being able to throw ourselves into this completely for God. We travelled many miles all over the country during that time, meeting all those who were at the hub of large-scale evangelism.

At one point we went to Guernsey for a crusade. We did not take the caravan this time, but flew there in a small Dakota aircraft. It was the first time any of us had flown, and we were very excited by the prospect. Unfortunately, Grace did not enjoy the experience very much, because for some reason it caused great pain in her ears, and we were all a little nervous when we saw that we had to land on Guernsey's simple grass runway! It seemed adequate for the job, however, and we landed safely.

We were met by our host, Mr. Ozanne, who was a local grower and member of the 'Guernsey States' Parliament. He lived in a beautiful farmhouse called 'Lilyvale', to where we were taken and introduced to his Scottish wife, Peggy, and daughter, Margaret.

We had been briefed beforehand that the family had recently experienced a tragedy, when their only son, Harry, had been killed in a car crash. The tragedy was all the more poignant because he had won a scholarship to study farming in Finland, and was just about to take it up in preparation for eventually taking over the family business. They were all still trying to come to terms with the disaster.

Margaret, who had studied nursing at the University College London, had been very close to her brother. After the accident she had returned to Guernsey, and was now reluctant to go back to her nursing, having become rather quiet and withdrawn. She had been encouraged to join the 'Youth For Christ' choir for this crusade, and we hoped the involvement might help her to adjust to life again.

We were welcomed enthusiastically, however, as Mrs. Ozanne set our first meal before us.

"Right. Stick in 'til you stick oot!" she laughed, with her characteristic Scottish accent.

The crusade really 'took off'. We all had a great time, and

many people were reached with the Gospel. The youth rallies were full of enthusiastic young people, one of which was a young man called John Blanchard, who was working in the legal department of the Courts of Guernsey. We had no idea then, that one day he would become the well-known international convention speaker. We also met a young singer with a beautiful deep bass voice. He, too, was as yet unheard of in wider circles. But a time would come when the voice of Peter Smith would be known by many.

I did, however, meet one man who was already well-known in Christian circles. The pianist, Jack Ward, attended some of the crusade meetings, and we played a duet or two together. Jack had already made many recordings by this time, and I was thrilled to have an opportunity to play the piano with him.

At the end of our time in Guernsey, we were tired, but exhilarated. The Ozannes thanked us for our part, and pressed us to return.

"Do come back," they urged. 'You would be welcome anytime."

And so we returned to the mainland, to go on with the increasing round of bookings. Most of the rallies and meetings in which we took part were usually events which had been planned as major projects for the churches or towns involved. This, however, did not always mean that we had good equipment to use. The absence of musically experienced folk in the churches usually showed in the condition of their pianos! Often, churches acquire their pianos through some kind of gift or bequest, and these are invariably a 'gift with strings attached'! They turn out to be pianos which no-one wants because they are beyond repair, and which cannot be got rid of for fear of offending the donor. I have experienced many of these 'gifts'!

One memorable example was in Neath, where the piano was so damp that I had to ask a man to stand by it to continually flick the hammers back so that they could be played again! Many pianos have missing notes, and one had nearly half of them unplayable!

They seemed very impressed with my efforts on the few available notes, however, and I was left wondering what their reaction would have been if I could have had a full complement!

On another occasion, I felt the 'sharps' and 'flats' (these are black notes to my sighted friends!) coming off as I played them. I could do no more but slip the loose notes in my top pocket so that they would not fall off the keyboard as I played! I had trouble getting them into my pocket by the time I was finished!

I played pianos in strange places, too! Once, we had a meeting on the lawn of a large house. The weather had been very wet, but everyone was pleased to see the sun come out just in time for the meeting. The piano was man-handled out into the garden - which probably did not do it a great deal of good - and it was placed on the lawn.

Unfortunately, they did not place it on boards, and as the meeting progressed, I felt the piano sinking further and further into the lawn. In the end, the pedals were flat against the grass and were unusable! Maybe they stopped it from disappearing altogether!

During our travels we met some wonderful people. We were usually overcome by the welcome we received, and the kind way in which our every need was anticipated. We gradually learned, however, to be careful what we said. There was, for instance, the occasion when Grace admired the beautiful cloth which was on the tea table. As soon as tea was over, our host shook the cloth, folded it and presented it to Grace. Another time, Grace passed a comment about a particularly lovely vase standing on the side-board. When the lady went out into the kitchen, I quietly said to Grace,

"You know, you shouldn't have said that - she'll be wrapping it up for you!"

"Surely not," said Grace, 'I was only being polite."

All went well, and the incident was forgotten. At the end of the evening, just as we were getting into the car to return to the caravan, the lady suddenly called out,

"Just a minute!" and dashed back into the house. A moment or two later she returned carrying the vase. "Here," she said, "since you liked it so much, please take it!" Grace never passed comments about the fittings and fixtures after that!

Anyone in full-time Christian service will know that they are never likely to be wealthy! We were never actually in want, though, because God's word says that he will provide all our needs if we trust him. We did trust Him for everything - even our clothes. At one point Grace was in great need of a warm coat. She did *not* acquire one by remarking on the exellent taste of one of our hostesses - no, we prayed about the need!

It was on one of our trips that we happened to stay with a Mrs. Pople - who remains a good friend to this day. For no apparent reason, she suddenly brought out a superb coat which she offered to Grace with some apprehension. With a gasp of astonishment, Grace cried,

"What an answer to prayer - it's just what I needed, and it's a perfect fit!"

We were all amazed, but it struck me that this reaction is typical of Christians - we pray for our needs as the Lord commands, and then we are surprised when the prayers are answered! I remarked,

"Why should you be be surprised? The Word says, '....their *sighs* went up to heaven.......'!"

There were some real characters in some of the places we visited. One dear old farmer in Somerset showed concern because we had a lot of rain during the campaign. It seemed as though it always began to rain directly before each meeting, and he was anxious that people were being put off attending. We used to have prayer meetings at 5.00am each morning to fit in with the milking, and at one of these he prayed:

"Lorrrd, oi wanna pray about the weather. You do know wass 'appnin'.....ev'ry nioght at seven a'clock it do start a'rainin'......in fac', Lord, we'm beginnin' ter wonder which side you'm on!"

A lady in Essex, left us wondering one day. She asked Reg: "Would yer like anuvver cuppa tea?"

"I don't think I can manage a full cup," said Reg, "can I just have half a cup?"

"A' course!" she said, but added, "are yer quite sure?" Reg assured her that he was, and off she went to the kitchen. A few minutes later she returned with the tea. The cup was absolutely brimming - it was spilling over into the saucer.

"Is that really alright?" she asked him worriedly, "yer could 'ave 'ad a full cup if yer'd wanted, y'know"!

There were so many lovely people and wonderful experiences. It was a time of fun and great fulfilment, but best of all, many people were reached with the good news of forgiveness for sin and new life in Jesus. It was a very busy time, and there were problems, of course, but we were very happy as we travelled around.

We had been just over two years in full-time Christian work, when Grace became very ill. Suddenly all our engagements were abruptly curtailed, and I was obliged to return home. Grace did eventually recover, although perhaps not completely, but we were unable to re-form our work, and I had to consider returning to the Birmingham workshops.

Grace and Reg were to have a very different destiny. Some time later, they went to Canada where Reg took on the Pastorate of a church, but it was to end in tragedy. They had a woman member of their congregation, who attended with her children. Sadly, the husband, who drank heavily, one day inexplicably burst into Grace and Reg's home, shot them both dead, then went on to shoot his wife and children, and finally, himself. This dreadful tragedy can only be left to God's sovereign will to explain. We can only know that they are now experiencing the eternal life which they preached about, and that one day we will all meet up again in Glory.

I took the change in my circumstances very badly. We were

doing so well and people were being saved. Why should God allow such a thing to happen? It seemed senseless.

I discussed the problem with a friend, Sid, who was one of the workshop tuners. I had been instrumental in his conversion when he came to our church and was initially impressed by the people who shook hands with him at the door. He had been a churchgoer, but he had never encountered the kind of vibrant Christianity he found at our church.

He was doubtful as to whether I could return to the workshops. Not so many tuners were needed now.

I did not know what to do, but I prayed about the problem. It was constantly on my mind, and as I carried in the coal for the fire one evening, I was still praying. "Lord," I begged, "what am I to do? I wanted so much to serve you, and now it's all gone."

Suddenly a Scripture came to me: 'This is the will of God, even your sanctification'. It hit me like a bomb! God was saying that although I wanted to be in the big time, the first thing he wanted from me was not my service but my separation to him. He wanted my commitment, so that however I served him, our relationship would be secure.

I realised that in all the work I had been doing for him, it hadn't done much for my relationship with him. This was to be a time of consolidation with God.

Chapter 12

BEGINNING TOGETHER

Illness was once more looming large in my life. Some time before Grace had been ill, we had all three had medical checks, and although, surprisingly, Grace's forthcoming illness was not foreseen, the doctor had spotted something in me. Apparently I had a congenital hiatus hernia which would lead to all sorts of complications as I grew older. I was going to have to submit to another operation sooner or later, and the doctor referred me to the hospital.

While I waited to be admitted, I applied to the Birmingham workshops, and in spite of the difficult economic climate, I was taken on again. I was therefore able to provide the vital financial support to my mother in my father's final illness.

The other tuners received me gracefully, and asked what I had been doing for the last couple of years and I was able to witness to them about going all over the country playing and preaching.

In the summer of 1960 another big crusade took place in Birmingham, this time with Eric Hutchings, and my mother actually made a decision for Christ, although she did not attend a fellowship and so never grew spiritually.

Then my father was taken into hospital again, and we knew that the lung cancer was now in its final stages.

Dad's brother, my uncle Bert, who had been a milkman when I was a child, was now in the blood transfusion service, and he could put on his white coat and pop in to see Dad at any time without waiting for visiting hours. One day, when Dad had realised that he was not going to recover, he poignantly asked Bert to take care of Lily (my mother) for him after he had gone.

We had all assumed that as he was always so ill with bronchitis and pleurisy in the winter time, that he would be bound to succumb to the cold eventually. However, true to my father's inborn sense of humour, he died on June 25th - the day after Midsummer's Day! It was also strange that two years before, uncle Bert's wife, (my auntie Mary) had also died on June 25th.

I received my call to be admitted to the Queen Elizabeth hospital, Birmingham, in August. When the surgeon came to see me before the operation, he had someone with him to whom he offered a few choice words of explanation.

"This man's eyes were shot to hell when he was a baby," he said.

Quickly I replied, 'Yes, and I won't be going there to fetch them!"

The operation was a massive one which included having to have several ribs sawn through to reach the hernia. When I came round afterwards, I felt very ill indeed, and was in great pain. My tuner friend, Sid, and his wife, Eileen, came to visit me, and my mother, of course, who was greatly helped by my uncle Bert. But Joe was also a frequent visitor, and he was so concerned to see how ill I was that he prayed for me often. I would probably be amazed to know just how often Joe prayed for me, and I thank God for the gift of one who still is the embodiment of a faithful friend.

As I was recovering in hospital, it was suggested that I go away for a time of convalescence. I wasn't very keen, but Sid and Eileen encouraged me by reminding me that I had always wanted to return to Guernsey. They suggested that they would enjoy a holiday in Guernsey to, and that Eileen would be pleased to help look after me.

So I typed a letter to Mr. and Mrs. Ozanne, and asked if a visit was possible. They wrote back to say that they were off to Canada for a holiday, but that their daughter, Margaret, would be remaining as she was working as a theatre nurse in the local hospital, and that we were welcome to come and fend for ourselves.

That was an excellent arrangement, and we fixed to stay for a week.

We had a wonderful time, and thoroughly enjoyed ourselves. On the Wednesday, we decided on an outing to Sark where we booked a pony and carriage for a trip around the island. However, every time the carriage jolted, I was conscious of a searing pain in my back which grew worse and worse. By the time we got back from Sark I was very much the worse for wear, and Margaret's uncle decided I should go to hospital.

They discovered that I had a stitch abscess which would have to be dressed each day while I was there, and then I would have to report back to the hospital in Birmingham. When we told Margaret about it, she immediately asked the doctor if she could attend to the dressing to save me having to keep on going into the hospital each day, and he readily agreed. So for the remainder of the week, Margaret looked after me very efficiently, and I was able to enjoy my holiday.

When the time came to leave, we bought Margaret a 'thankyou' box of chocolates, which she delightedly accepted by saying,

"These are lovely! You've picked the ones I like - I'm not normally a *sweet lover*!"

Of course, Sid made as much of that as possible, and Margaret's blushes were cloaked in gales of laughter!

At home, the hospital confirmed the stitch abscess, and this set back my recovery for some time. It was well into the Autumn before I was able to work again, but another surprise was in store for me.

At an appropriate moment, my mother sat down to speak to me.

"Your uncle Bert has asked me to marry him," she began

tentatively.

All I could think of was "Whatever did you say?"

"I told him I would have to ask you first," she replied.

Non-plussed again, I simply asked "Why?"

"Because," said my mother, taking a deep breath, "this is your home and we would have to move house to Hamsworth on the other side of Birmingham."

I was grateful for her concern about me, but I really could not see any problem. I assured her that I felt it would be the finest thing for both of them. I liked uncle Bert. He was a jovial character and comfortable to be with. He compared favourably with my father whose illness had often made him morose. Uncle Bert was always in good health, and as a milkman, he had often called in to our home with his cheery greetings. Once he had even given me the princely sum of two shillings and sixpence! I certainly approved of Uncle Bert! He was a nice man and I was all for a closer relationship.

Their wedding was a lovely occasion, and I am one of the few people who can say that I played at my mum's wedding! But my mother was even more unique because she not only married two brothers and therefore did not change her name, but she also eventually had two silver weddings! The Birmingham Evening Mail got to hear of it years later, and took pictures of her on her eightieth birthday.

In the summer of 1961, Sid, Eileen and myself took another trip to Guernsey and spent a lovely week with Margaret as she showed us the sights. We saw the underground hospital, the shell chapel, and lots of other places - many of which were connected with the German occupation, and had now become tourist attractions.

We also made the short trip across the Channel to Dinard, where we made the mistake of ordering a 'menu gastronomique' in a restaurant.

Unfortunately, this was the most gigantic meal possible, and since I was still recovering from the operation of the year before,

I could not manage a quarter of the meal! But we laughed and enjoyed ourselves enormously.

It was during this week that I began to realise that I was going to miss Margaret a great deal when the visit was over. She was due to visit friends in Kent later in the year, and she asked me how far Kent was from Birmingham.

"Oh, just a couple of train rides," I answered truthfully, not mentioning how long were the rides!

At the end of October, she came to visit us in Hamsworth, and soon became completely at home with Mum and Uncle Bert. Like everyone else, they loved her easy nature and quiet, loving ways. It would be difficult not to like Margaret.

On the day I asked her to marry me, I carefully listed all the 'cons'.

"You know that I have serious limitations," I warned. 'I can't paper the walls or paint the ceilings, and I won't be able to drive or even navigate for you."

But Margaret brushed all my arguments aside with the comment: 'Well, I know a lot of men who wouldn't paper the walls or paint the ceilings even if they could, so we won't worry about that!"

So we decided to get engaged at Christmas, and although I hated to see her return to Guernsey, I was left feeling that maybe, at last there was hope for the future.

It was only a week or two later that my 'future' nearly came to an abrupt end.

On November 5th, I was coming back from a meeting in Northfield. My driver, Winston, was also a singer who had taken part in the meeting. He was an excellent soloist who had been a Carol Levis 'discovery' in the radio days before television's 'Opportunity Knocks'. He would say 'Carol Levis discovered me, but Jesus Christ recovered me'!

On the way home we gave someone else a lift, dropping him off at Winson Green. Since I was in the back seat, Winston asked if I would like to change to the front now. As there was not far to go, I decided to stay where I was.

We were just crossing a junction on the outer ring road, when a car came hurtling from a side road and smashed into our car. We swung violently around, and hit a tree.

The car was a total write-off, with the nearside door completely ripped away and shredded. If I had been sitting in that front seat I would undoubtedly have been killed or seriously injured. I was taken to hospital for observation having lacerations to my arm and an eye, and a possible broken rib. Miraculously, the side on which I had had the operation was undamaged.

News got to Margaret in Guernsey, and remembering her brother's death in a car crash, I wanted to assure her that I was all right, so arranged to fly over on the 25th November.

There seemed little point in waiting until Christmas to announce our engagement, so I bought a ring and slipped it onto her finger at a romantic moment as we were listening to the third movement of Brahms beautiful piano concerto - thereby making it forever very special to us.

Both our families were overjoyed at the news, and our future happiness was assured.

We were married on June 6th 1962, and had planned an 'away from it all' honeymoon. My life had become a constant round of meeting people and speaking at crowded gatherings, and it seemed now, that wherever I went I would come across someone who knew me.

We would ensure at least one week of quiet and privacy before I had to begin it all again. The ideal place would be Switzerland - Margaret had always wanted to go there and it would be a place where I could remain anonymous. We decided on the Christian hotel, 'Rosat', in the village of Chateau d'Oex, in the Bernese Oberland, for a week's honeymoon.

As we walked into the hotel, I mentioned to Margaret:

"Well, now we are completely away from everything and everybody who know us!"

We had not reached the end of the foyer before a man came

up and said:

"Hello, Margaret! How lovely to see you!" He was a friend from Guernsey who had married the hotel proprietor's daughter! I was amazed! Particularly because it was Margaret - quiet Margaret, who liked to stay away from the limelight, who was the one who was known!

The next morning, like true honeymooners, we had our breakfast in our room, and there came a knock on the door. In my best French I called 'Entre', and in walked a girl who said:

"Hello, Mr. Jackson, I'm Christine Winterburn. Do you remember - you came to our church to do a gospel campaign in 1958?" The world is, indeed, a small place!

It was a lovely week. Even in June there was still snow in the sunshine and we climbed mountains - in a cable car, of course! But we managed to extend our week for one extra day when we completely failed to realise that we were supposed to change trains on the journey home. Instead of arriving at Geneva, we found ourselves at Frieburg, and by the time we got to our destination, our plane had gone! So we had to spend a night in London with some obliging friends, and travel on home the following day.

Home, to begin with, was a room in the house of my mother and uncle Bert.

We began looking for a house of our own straight away, but we were grateful for the chance of being together while we took our time to search for the right place. The only problem was that we were a long way from our church. It meant that we were rather cut off from the mid-week meetings and the many friends we had made there.

We did have one good friend, however, who lived near us. I had known Geoff Bowater for a long time, and had enjoyed many a time of fellowship with him and his family.

Geoff began to express concern that the Shirley area of Birmingham had no suitable place of worship, and together we began to think and pray about what should be done. We knew of a few 'disembodied' Christians - those who were not members of any existing church - who lived in the area, and we began to think about getting them together and forming a completely new fellowship.

In October 1963, the work began with our first meeting of eleven people in the Shirley Institute, because, of course, we had no building of our own. It was hard, pioneering work, but we prayed a lot, and the fellowship gradually began to grow. It was a lovely experience to see new members from time to time, and the zeal for God's work kindled in each new heart.

At the same time, Margaret and I were looking for a home of our own. Eventually we found one which we felt was just 'us', and we were soon able to move in. It was just across the road from our friends, Geoff and Winnie Bowater, and we were delighted with it, although we had to spend some time - and money - enlarging the kitchen.

I began to realise that it is one thing to have enough money to look after myself, but quite another to keep two of us and a home! I would have to think about becoming selfemployed. It might be that I could earn more this way.

An appointment was therefore made with the management of the workshops, and I explained my intentions to them. They were very helpful to me, suggesting that I joined their 'homeworkers' scheme. It was an incredibly fair - and in those days - trusting scheme, which meant that I would tell them what I earned each week, and they would make it up to a minimum wage until I got onto my feet.

At first it was a struggle to find enough work, but then I had a break when a large city store asked me to maintain all their pianos. This gave me one full day's permanent work each week, and provided a little security.

Gradually work began to come in, and soon the Birmingham authority did not have to make up my wages at all, except for ensuring that I had a wage when I was on holiday. They really looked after me very well indeed, and I will always be grateful for their support.

Our new church fellowship plodded on slowly. Then we had a breakthrough. The famous Arthur Blessit came to Birmingham. Arthur was a typical guy of the nineteen-sixties - a drop-out from society, who had thrown off society's constraints to 'do his own thing'. But the difference between him and other 'drop-outs' was that he had found Christ, and was fully committed to serving him. This outrageous personality who didn't seem to care what anyone thought about the way he looked or dressed, attracted many young people, but directed them persistently toward the Lord Jesus.

After his visit, a lot of young people came into our church fellowship, and the work really 'took off'. These young people who were confused by the contradictions of life, were looking for answers. They found them, like so many others have done, in the person of the Lord Jesus Christ, and their lives suddenly found meaning.

From this point on, our fellowship grew, and we soon needed a building of our own.

So we applied to the council for a building plot. After much consultation, we were disappointed to learn that there were no plots available, but we continued to pray.

Some time later, two ladies, who heard that we were looking out for somewhere to build a church, came to us and mentioned that they knew of a free plot.

"It is right beside Shirley Railway Station," they said, 'and we claimed it for God twenty years ago!"

They had simply seen it, and noticed it's potential as a site for a work of God, and had repeatedly 'claimed' it by prayer in God's name.

Soon we had appointed a Christian solicitor to negotiate with the council for us, and this time there were no obstacles. The plot was ours, and Shirley Evangelical Church was founded.

Very shortly afterwards, the solicitor died. Our project was one of the last transactions he made.

Today, the church has two or three hundred members and Geoff's son, Anthony is the Pastor. His other son, Chris, is the well-known Christian song writer.

But now my piano tuning business was becoming very busy, and I had to travel around the area widely - alone.

I was quite used to using public transport to get myself from place to place, and found most people willing to lend me a hand if I needed one. Not that I often needed help, of course. I could cope much better than most people seemed to think! In fact, it has always amazed me that so many who can see where they are going perfectly well, seem to get into a panic when they are on a train, in case they go past their stop!

Knowing my exact whereabouts has never been a problem to me at all - with the possible exception of that little incident on the return journey from our honeymoon - and that was entirely different! However, I had to admit that I did have the occasional collision, and then when I fell down a manhole.........

Chapter 13

AN OPEN DOOR

Training for my guide dog took place at Leamington Spa, one of several centres then, but in recent years many more have been added. Any potential guide dog handler is required to spend up to four weeks learning how to control and look after a dog, before getting a dog of their own.

Training guide dogs is a highly organised - and yet still privately funded - venture. It takes around £2,500 to train one guide dog, all of which comes from voluntary contributions of one kind and another.

The dogs, mainly labradors and labrador/golden retriever crosses, with alsatians not used quite so often nowadays, are chosen from specially bred puppies for their character and suitability for training. They then spend nine or ten months with a 'puppy walker', learning the rudiments of obedience, and becoming acclimatised to all kinds of different situations. The association has nearly eight hundred puppies in preparation, of which about eighty percent will become guide dogs. When they are ready, they go to a centre for nine month's serious training.

Now they begin to learn specific skills - how to respond to certain commands which will indicate which direction they must take, how to avoid obstacles - taking into account the height and width of their owner - and how to deal with traffic. The dog learns to wear a harness - a handled framed which gives him freedom of movement, and through which his owner can sense his actions. Before long he realises that as soon as the harness is in place, he is on duty, and his behaviour must reflect that fact.

The dog does not instinctively know what is expected of him, and he learns by discipline and encouragement. Should the dog forget what he must do, he is reminded by a sharp command and a tug on the harness, but when he remembers, he is rewarded with a loving pat or display of affection. Dogs respond to love and will usually willingly obey if they understand and know they are appreciated.

When the appropriate standard has been reached, the dog is ready to meet his potential owner. By this time, the owner will have completed his training too, and they begin to get to know each other and whether they are compatible. The staff at the centre will have completed a surprisingly in-depth research into the blind person's character and habits - even style of walking - in order to match him or her with the right dog.

The owner too, has to learn. He discovers that very strict rules must be obeyed if his dog is to remain healthy and happy, and therefore able to serve efficiently. One rule is regarding meals. The dog must have only one good meal each day, of a prescribed content, together with a measure of biscuit. He must *never* be fed between meals! This often proves difficult for the blind owner when good-intentioned individuals try to offer the dog biscuits or even sweets while he is on duty. It is not only bad for the dog, but it distracts his attention from his job and can prove dangerous.

My dog was a beautiful pale yellow labrador called Donna, and we became inseparable. I used to say that she was the only ash-blonde I would ever leave home with! She joined me soon after I got the tuning contract with the Birmingham store, and before long she was well known amongst the employees and customers. Unfortunately, the pianos I had to tune were on the same floor as the restaurant, and Donna used to sit at the door and wait patiently for me to finish.

However, the people who were eating in the restaurant seemed to want to show their interest by feeding Donna with all sorts of scraps, and although she undoubtedly accepted their offerings with relish, it could not be allowed to continue. Then someone had an idea. They rang the advertising department, and before long Donna could be seen sitting patiently again, but with a very smart and prominent notice above her head saying: 'Please do not feed the dog'! Her days of indulgence were over.

During one of these days, I happened to meet a young man whom I knew from one of the churches which Grace, Reg and I visited from time to time. He was studying Behavioural Science at Aston University, and had taken time off for lunch.

We happily greeted one another, and as neither of us had eaten, we decided to take advantage of the restaurant and extend our chat over a meal. This became a regular lunch time appointment, and we both looked forward to a break in our work to meet up each Friday in the store restaurant.

One day, as we were chatting, he told me that he had been assigned to lead the worship at the church on a particular Sunday. He did not know why he was chosen - he said he just took his turn. But after the service, a lady called to him.

"That was very good," she said. "You sing well and have a gift for leading worship!"

My young friend was bemused by this, and recounted it to me incredulously.

"Develop it!" I ordered him. "If you have a gift - develop it!"

He did, and some time later, a group was formed called 'The Alethians', who went on to be a blessing to many with their very popular music at missions, outreaches and services, and also in recordings.

That was not the end of the matter, however. Another landmark occurred when I mentioned to my friend that I had been invited to take up full-time Christian work. He was struck by this idea, and began to pray that God would show him whether this was something which he should think about too. From this beginning, the Holy Spirit led him on to develop a ministry which has blessed thousands, right through to the eventual formation of 'The Saltmine Trust'. The worship leadership and singing of Dave Pope has become known and loved by many over a good many years.

I was honoured to be used by God in this small way to set Dave on to the work God had planned for him, but it also impressed me that what we say to people may have a lasting effect on their lives. How important are our words!

My alliance with Donna proved beneficial in many ways. She was an unfailing friend on journeys, but her gentle, affectionate nature made her very popular with everyone, and I began to use her as a living parable in my preaching. It was easy to show in her, a picture of the pleasures of obedience and the perils of disobedience in our daily walk with God.

She could also be the means of contact with someone who needed to hear about the love of God. Like the man I met one day when I was walking with Donna to a bus stop on the way home. He approached us and surprisingly asked:

"Can I walk with you?"

I agreed, and for a while we chatted. He made approving comments about this and that and how good Donna was, and he asked me questions about my blindness, (as I often find happens). I was able to assure him that I had no regrets about being blind because I lived such a full life. When we reached the bus stop, he gripped my hand fervently, and I thanked him.

"No," he remonstrated. "I want to thank you. When I came up to you, I was thinking of taking my life, but meeting you has made me think again."

When I got on the bus I was dizzy with amazement. What would have happened if I had taken his overtures as an offer of unnecessary help, and asserted my independence? So often blind people have to cope with patronising attention in the name of good intentions, and I could have easily rebuffed him. I was so glad I had reacted sensitively, and mentally chalked it up for future reference.

The greater part of my job with the store in Birmingham consisted of after sales. On one occasion I had to go to the home of a lady in Sutton Coldfield, who had just had a new piano delivered. I had limited time because I was due back to a children's afternoon meeting in Shirley, so I got on with the job steadily. Suddenly the lady said:

"Excuse me mentioning it, but you look so peaceful and happy - why is that?"

"Why do you ask?" I hedged.

"Well," she went on, "how can you be so happy? Tell me the secret."

Now I have never felt it right to use my condition or my access into people's homes as a tool for evangelism *per se*. I am convinced that forcing the issue puts off more people than it attracts. My way has always been to allow God room to move. If he leads me to someone who needs a word at the right moment, then he will prompt them to speak and give me the opportunity to reply. This seemed like one of those occasions, but I still wanted to be sure.

"Do you have a Bible?" I asked. This would give her a chance to close the conversation if she wished.

"Yes," she said eagerly, "I'll get it!"

"Do you really want to know?" I persisted. If at this point she was still interested, then I could go ahead without being accused of 'ramming home religion'.

She assured me she wanted me to go on, and I told her that the Bible was the answer.

"It presents the one who is giving me this happiness," I said.

She was suddenly disappointed. "It's no good for me," she said sadly. "I suppose you are going to tell me to come to Christ....... well, I can't, because I'm living with a man who is not my husband. I'm waiting for a divorce - my husband walked out on me, and now Joe and I are waiting to get married."

Once again I was faced with a dilemma. I knew that many of my Christian colleagues - particularly some of the older ones - would have enforced orthodox Christianity and told the lady with a frown that she must remove herself from the sin before coming to Christ. Instead, I said,

"Turn to Luke 5, verse 11." The beauty of being blind is that if they turn to something, they have to read it! They are more likely to remember it that way!

She read, "A man full of leprosy came to Jesus."

"Stop right there!" I said. 'This man did not try to get rid of his problem - he came *with* it. You are full of your problem. Jesus transformed this man's life and he will transform yours - if you are willing. Jesus also said 'Are you willing?' and *then*, 'Be clean'.

The next time I went to see Gill, she greeted me with the news,

"Jesus has come into my life! When you left last time I went into the kitchen and prayed that Jesus would touch me. Since then I also met a lady who welcomed me into a fellowship and now I meet with them regularly!"

"What about Joe?" was my next question.

"I would love to reach him for Christ," said Gill, "but he is Hungarian, and cannot read my English Bible."

Before I left, we had decided on a plan whereby I would write to a publisher for Hungarian literature, and while she waited for it to arrive, I asked her to pray that she would have wisdom to know when the time was right to speak to Joe. Soon after, Joe suffered a stroke and had to go into hospital. He could only lie on his back, and his reading was very limited.

Gill visited, and each time left one of the small testimony leaflets which she had received, about how Christ had changed people's lives. Joe was pleased to read them in his own language, and soon wanted to read the gospel that Gill had also received.

Next time I saw them, Joe had been saved, and they were planning their wedding. Eventually even Gill's son by her first marriage became a Christian, and he went on to be a man of God. If I had been too orthodox, Gill would probably have been lost, and so would her family.

(I never did get to the children's meeting!)

In 1965 we had a phone call which caused us some excitement. The call came from Ben Peake of the Movement for World

Evangelisation. (MWE) This was an organisation which had been founded in 1931 for the purpose of spreading the gospel of Christ, and was now heading crusades and a Bible teaching ministry in many parts of the world. They were also the well-known organisers in England of the highly successful annual convention at Filey in Yorkshire which was attended by hundreds of Christians.

Ben told me that they had a team touring Portugal, taking meetings and doing personal work. He mentioned some of the evangelists which I had heard about - Dave Foster, whose speciality was to draw instant pictures with board and chalk; Frank Farley and Don Summers - both powerful speakers; and a young man called Peter Smith who was the soloist. He had a remarkable deep, rich, bass voice which reminded us of the singing of George Beverley Shea, the soloist for Billy Graham. Ben went on to say that their musician couldn't complete the tour, and they were looking for another pianist. He wondered if I could join them.

This was a wonderful opportunity, and Margaret and I happily agreed to go for three weeks.

The tour was hectic, but fun. We travelled to many parts of Portugal, taking large and small meetings. All the preaching was done through interpreters, of course, and this required some practise. It is only when someone is translating your every word that you begin to realise how many colloquialisms and vernacular sayings you use. Even Peter Smith's songs were translated, and the problem was noticeable when he sang 'Swing Low, Sweet Chariot'.

The translator couldn't handle it and was non-plussed. Deciding on an alternative he announced: "Swing low, sweet donkey cart"!

The final part of the tour was to Faro. We were there to give testimonies of what the Lord had done for us, and to lead worship with our music. On our way back to Lisbon, we had to undertake a four to five hour journey, and were met my our host and hostess who took us on to their club for a meal.

I had not eaten very well in Portugal, somehow the food did not agree with me, but the sweet on this occasion was delicious. It was pineapple floating in madeira wine, and I had not had anything like it before. I demolished it with relish. My hostess, seeing how much I had enjoyed her choice, asked me if I would like more. It was irresistible. I had to say "yes, please," and another huge helping of the delicious confection was placed before me.

When I got up, I found I was swaying, and had to lean on Margaret.

"Take it easy," she advised me, 'but whatever you do, don't start singing!"

They took us then to see the sights, but I saw nothing - I was sound asleep in the back of the car!

1967 was another landmark for us. It was then that we discovered that we were expecting our first baby. We were very excited, and were quite sure that it would be a boy. We thought about names - boy's names - and since we favoured something Biblical, we decided upon 'Timothy'. We felt it would be nice if his second name was something Scottish, since all Margaret's relatives on her mother's side were Scottish. So we chose 'Fraser', and 'Timothy Fraser' was duly born on May 8th, 1968.

I will never forget the wonderful experience of hearing his first cry, and holding the tiny baby in my arms. It was magic!

We were quite besotted by him, as I suppose most new parents are about their firstborn, and we cooed and fussed accordingly.

I did not take a large part in the practical side of caring for Tim, but a few months after he was born, Margaret hinted that she particularly wanted to go to a missionary meeting at the church. In fact, she hinted for the entire week, until I quipped that you have to be 'hintelligent' to hear hints!

I was therefore left with Tim, but it did not turn out to be easy. The first half hour was fine, but then I heard a cry from the pram.

132

I dropped everything - (which was a pity because I was drying up at the time!) - and went into the dining room, where he had been settled into his pram.

"Never fear, daddy's here!" I called, and processed him round the room. This had no effect and he continued to cry. I went on to try everything I could think of including trying to feed him, but nothing would settle him. I patted appropriate parts of his anatomy - which made an interesting percussion instrument - but it was to no avail. My frustration grew, and I remembered a song which went, 'Art thou troubled? Sweet music shall calm thee.......'

So I took him into the front room where the piano was, placed him in his carry cot, and proceeded to play him some Chopin. It had a good effect for a few minutes - it was part of Chopin's 'Funeral March'; but during those few minutes, he summoned all the remaining energies of his tiny frame, and raised a cry which was destined to reach Margaret who was four miles away! I snatched him from his cot and retreated to the back of the house.

"Timothy Fraser," I remonstrated, "What am I going to do with you?" And composed a song to help the cause.......

Timothy Fraser, it's time to go to bed,

Timothy Fraser, remember what we said,

Timothy Fraser, if you don't we'll bash your head!........

(The music to this silly song seems to have gone down into posterity, and is often asked for even now, wherever I go!)

Another thought struck me. Beyond our garden was the back garden of a nursing home and I did think of renting him out for a while, but if Margaret came home early it would take some explaining!

Suddenly it occurred to me that it must be getting darker. Of course! That was the trouble! Tim was afraid of the dark, and he had become more frightened as each hour passed. I swtiched on the light, and wonder of wonders! - peace reigned immediately!

I had tried to soothe him, feed him, scold him, love him - but all he needed was light.

When Margaret returned and asked how my evening had been, I recounted the story. I have been doing so ever since, because I recognised in the experience, the great truth that men and women, and boys and girls everywhere, who are distressed by the results of sin in their lives, will find themselves transformed by the light of the Gospel of Jesus Christ.

All they need is *light*.

Chapter 14

THE WORK EXPANDS

As I travelled around I often came across blind people who were almost confined to their homes for one reason or another. Some had other handicaps which hampered their mobility, others found it difficult to adjust to blindness perhaps because they had become blind later in life. For those of us who had never known any other kind of life, the condition was normal, and we developed as full a life-style as any sighted person. However, being blind can cause a tendency to introversion, and I came across many blind folk who created a life revolving around themselves which seemed to try to shut out the world around them.

I began to develop an idea which I hoped might help to alleviate this problem in some small way. It seemed to me that fellowship groups might possibly be formed which could cater for blind people, but at the same time would interest sighted folk. They could serve several purposes:

Firstly, I wanted to reach people - particularly blind people - with the gospel. These were the ones I called 'twice blind'. They were blind both physically and spiritually. Secondly, I wanted to widen their horizons by helping them to cope in a better way in the world. But at the same time, integration would help sighted people to obtain a more balanced view of the blind.

Blindness is a very emotive subject to most people, and often they have no idea how to handle it when they come across it. They are usually anxious to help, but do not know how or when to offer assistance. Some sighted folk will offer more help than is needed, making the blind person feel patronised, others will feel that they must not help until asked, and then suffer confusion and even guilt when they think they have not helped when they should! On any account, the situation is difficult for both blind and sighted alike - when they are not used to being together. My answer was in integration, so that both blind and sighted could get to understand each other.

It was to this end, therefore, that the first fellowship group was set up in Birmingham. It began with a large group of between forty and fifty mostly blind people, and pioneered a format which most subsequent groups would adopt. There was a Transport Officer who would see that all who could not get to the venue on their own were brought in by some means; a secretary who dealt with the copious paperwork, a treasurer, and a prayer co-ordinator who would liase with the local churches. The meeting would begin with a roll-call. This was important so that everyone could get to know who was there; and the meeting would go on to include some hymns (using Braille hymn books); a short devotional talk, and it would finish with tea. It was known as 'The Torch Fellowship'; a name adopted because many of the blind members were associated with an organisation known as 'The Torch Trust', which operated from a large house at Hurstpierpoint in Sussex.

My first contact with 'Torch' had been at school where a magazine used to mysteriously appear every so often. It had big embossed letters which we could feel with our fingers on the front cover saying 'The Torch', and when we opened it we could feel the words in Braille. It was a little evangelical magazine giving a short story and an illustration from the Bible.

'Torch Trust' had been founded in 1931 mainly by a Miss Trench, but had been taken over in 1958 by Ron and Stella Heath, when the work began to prosper. Now they were beginning to reach people in all parts of the world with literature in Braille, and in the new ministry of cassette tapes.

My taste of full-time Christian service once again, through the experiences in Portugal had made me feel a bit restive in my spirit, although I was very busy tuning pianos. I became increasingly interested in the work of the Torch Trust for the blind, and in 1969 I went down to their National Thanksgiving service. As I listened to the reports and heard about the excellent job they were doing, I realised that my vision might possibly be an extension of the work of the Torch Trust, and that here might be an opening back into the full time Christian ministry which I had missed.

My involvement with Torch began slowly. I discussed my ideas with Ron and Stella, and I shared with them my vision about spreading the gospel to my fellow blind people. The work of Torch was wonderful, but it was evangelism at arm's length, and my aim was to take it a step further to bring the blind out of their homes and into the community together with sighted people.

The second fellowship group was formed in Leicester, while I was still earning my living at tuning pianos. But then there was a breakthrough.

I received another telephone call from Ben Peake of MWE. He told me that they were anxious to put together a full-time ministry team, consisting of evangelists and musicians.

"Your help in Portugal was very successful," he said, "and now we have Eric Clarke as a soloist. We would like you to consider joining us in a full-time capacity, as accompanist and evangelist."

I was very interested, but I had to be honest about my hopes.

"This is something I would just love to do, but I have something else. I'm beginning to be involved with 'Torch Trust'."

He suggested we got together to talk over the matter, and we agreed to meet at the Swiss Centre Restaurant in Leicester Square for lunch.

In all my travels, I had never before eaten in such an illustrious place as the Swiss Centre, so my journey to London was undertaken with some excitement. Then, when I walked through the door and felt the deep pile of the carpet beneath my feet, my heart took a jump! I briefly wondered why I should feel so nervous - this was, after all, simply a restaurant, and there were merely people eating in it!

We ordered our lunch, and then got down to business. Ben began by asking me,

"Now then, what's your vision?"

I told him that first and foremost I wanted to reach my fellow blind people with the gospel.

"Splendid!" said Ben. 'We would like to help you in that. But what about Torch? Do you think they are in a position to support you financially full-time?"

I was sure that they had not thought about that at all.

"Right," Ben continued, "please pray about coming with us full-time, or even part-time with both. How about coming to our conference at Hildenborough Hall, and we can pray and share the vision with our council?"

This I did, and by the following May, in 1970, I was a full-time evangelist with the Movement for World Evangelisation.

I had been sad to release my ties with Geoff Bowater and the Shirley Evangelical Church, and knew that my going would leave Geoff with a greater burden. He was very gracious, however, and assured me that he was not a bit surprised - he did not think any one church could keep me for long!

I was now working under two banners, essentially with MWE, but they were quite happy for me to continue the fellowship projects with Torch. I would be available for MWE's crusades, meetings or other business, but I was free to travel around and set up fellowship groups for Torch at other times.

In September, 1970, I played for my first convention at Filey, in Yorkshire. Each year, Butlin's Holiday Camp was taken over by MWE as the venue for this very popular convention, and it became the highlight of each year for many Christians, as thousands met to praise God and learn more about the Christian life.

I was to continue playing for the Filey convention for a good number of years both under the banner of MWE and later independently, but eventually the convention came to an end when Butlin's finally closed down. There was a brief attempt to recreate 'Filey at Skegness', but it was never quite the same, and the convention has re-emerged in a slightly different form in the 'New Horizons' gatherings, which are now particularly successful in Northern Ireland.

Everything has to change, but I will always remember the electric atmosphere of those huge meetings, when hundreds of voices were raised in praise to God as they waited in eager anticipation to hear what he would have to say to them.

My work load increased alarmingly. In January 1971 I made my first trip to Northern Ireland where I assisted John Blanchard with a coffee bar mission for MWE. One of my earliest memories of these visits is the welcome I got from a minister friend in Ballymena. He announced to the congregation: "Peter reminds me of a budgie with no teeth - he was born to *succeed*!"

This may have been the first joke I heard in Ireland - it was not the last. I have probably heard more jokes in Ireland than anywhere else, and during each visit I acquire more to add to my already considerable store.

An Irish man once told me, "My favourite book is a dictionary - it tells you the meaning of the words as you go along!"

Another one told me about the Irish doctor talking to his patient. He said,

"I've got bad news and dreadful news - the bad news is that you have only twenty-four hours to live."

"That's terrible!" said the patient, "what's the dreadful news?"

"I should have told you yesterday," said the doctor!

My visit to Ireland ended just in time for me to return home for the birth of our second son, Christopher, on the 19th January.

There was a postal strike the following day, and we always said how glad we were to have our 'male' delivered on time! But in February I was back in Belfast forming another Torch Fellowship group!

Wearing my 'Torch' hat, I would go to a place where they were interested in forming a prayer cell in preparation for setting up a fellowship group. Having got the prayer going, I would then contact the Social Services to introduce myself and my aims, telling them that I wanted to integrate the blind with the sighted from the point of view of introducing them to the Christian faith.

The reaction I got was mixed and sometimes it could be blatantly hostile. There were two schools of thought. One was that the blind might be patronised, the other that the blind themselves might exploit their disability. In my case, I suppose some may have thought that I was exploiting my own disability in order to press home Christianity. To some extent this may be true - but for the highest motives!

It is certainly true that bringing Christ to the blind was and still is, my main aim. I have discovered personally how Christ can bring meaning to the emptiest of lives, and have experienced the life-changing difference the living God can make. In this, I did indeed hope that I could identify with other blind people and through the example of my own life, influence theirs.

But my interest was not only with the blind. I coveted all people for God, and wanted to bring Christ to anyone who would listen, but it was obvious that I would have an affinity with the blind.

On the whole, the Social Services were helpful . In the afternoons I would visit clubs for the blind, or maybe visit those who had recently gone blind, or lived alone. In the evenings I would spend time with representatives from the local churches, alerting them to the possibility of the formation of a fellowship group, so that they could play a part if they wished. In this way, my time quickly became very precious as my diary filled up.

MWE were very good in providing me with a realistic salary,

but with two young children and a mortgage to support, like many others we struggled to keep our heads above water. But God works in mysterious ways, and he had a plan in mind for us.

One of the groups I was helping to form was in Tunbridge Wells, Kent. While I was there, I stayed with three maiden lady sisters, the Misses Fraser. One of them worked at the National Westminster Bank, one had at one time been a governess/housekeeper for a professional family, but the other was deaf and blind.

Elsie, Hilda and Maggie Fraser were all committed Christians, and eager for God's work to be advanced, and they did all they could to prove it by making my job as easy as possible whilst I remained with them. One of the things which we have often laughed about since, happened when I first played on their piano. They were so anxious to help that they made all the usual mistakes in dealing with someone who is blind. This time, as I sat down on the piano stool, I felt one of the sisters pick up my hand, place it on the keyboard and separating my index finger, place it carefully on one of the centre keys.

"This is 'middle C'," she told me, confident that she had done her part to orient me properly! I didn't embarrass her by telling her that I didn't need orientation when I took a piano to pieces, repaired all its parts and put them back together again!

However, these dear ladies proved their concern for my welfare, and their commitment to God when they approached me one morning with a very special question. I was having breakfast, and was aware of the two sighted sisters, Elsie and Hilda, taking up positions on either side of me. I knew they must have something on their minds and after a little shuffling and clearing the throat, one spoke.

"We believe that God is telling us that we have to pay off your mortgage," she said.

I was stunned and didn't know what to say. Before I could think what to answer, she continued,

"Please ask your bank to let us know what your mortgage is,

and we'll settle it."

And that was the end of the matter. Nothing I could say would change their minds - they knew that God had spoken, and they intended to obey. Margaret and I will always be grateful to these Godly ladies who made a major contribution to our daily lives through their incredible generosity, because they were open to God's leading in the most surprising ways.

To some extent due to their help, I was able to continue in this work for seven years, and in that time over seventy fellowship groups were formed. And so my life became one long round of meetings, crusades, visits to fellowship groups already formed, and travels to new places where groups were needed.

At the same time there were also the house-parties. These were holiday times at least a week long, and usually several weeks, at which I would be responsible for the music, and some of the speaking - sometimes all of it - for the whole holiday. Although the accommodation in those early days was rather spartan, there is no doubt that the fellowship was great, and wonderful times of rest, relaxation and revival were enjoyed by all.

We had houseparties in all kinds of places - North Wales, Devon and even Switzerland, and they all went towards making my work load very heavy indeed. I was incredibly busy, and attempting to keep all my various projects going at once. Sometimes I had to make almost impossible arrangements in order to keep up with things.

Once when I was travelling to Scotland via the East Side of the country, I wanted very much to visit the folk who were forming the Newcastle-on-Tyne Torch Fellowship Group. The only way it could be done was for me to arrange to be met from the train in mid-journey, and have lunch with the group spearheader on the station platform! Then after lunch, I continued on to Scotland.

Margaret tried to make me understand that I was doing too much when, on one of my increasingly rare visits home, she asked me what I would like for lunch.

"Oh, anything," I replied, "you know I'm the easiest person to get along with!"

"Then give me the chance to find out!" she retorted, tersely.

But at a crusade in Guildford in 1972, I was to meet someone who would make me stop and take stock of my lifestyle.

Mr. Godden was a second-in command with the Inland Revenue - a busy man who knew what an all-encompassing job could do to a man. I stayed with him and his wife for the length of the crusade, and we chatted at length about my work. It was clear from what I told him that I was away from home far more that I was there, and he listened quietly.

Finally, one morning he leaned across the breakfast table, and as I hurried to get away to my next appointment he said:

" 'He knoweth our frame, he remebereth that we are dust' - it is *we* that forget!"

This really spoke to me. I took it as a 'word in season', and resolved to act upon it.

Chapter 15

EVEN HIGHER PROFILE

1972 promised to be every bit as hectic as the year before. In fact, with the work expanding, I was likely to have to spread myself even wider. As I rushed into the now familiar pattern, I remembered Mr. Godden's words. I could not keep up the present pace. Something would have to be done. After much consideration, I went to my friends at MWE. I told them that although I was extremely grateful for the support and freedom they had given me to continue my work with both themselves and Torch, I felt that now I was really not being very fair to them. My time was increasingly devoted to Torch, and yet I was being paid by MWE. I said that I really ought to be in full-time work with Torch who had been suggesting that I become their regional adviser.

Their reaction was kind, and indeed, gratifying. They pleaded with me to reconsider. They felt that I was making a mistake and that they had no complaints with my shared workload. They begged me to stay with them.

The decision was a difficult one to make, but I felt it was right to leave, and reluctantly they agreed to release me.

That summer, therefore, I began full-time work with Torch, and launched into a new pattern of mostly committee meetings as I directed the work of the now numerous fellowship groups all over the country.

I still travelled widely, of course, and it was travelling 'heavy' - not light! I could not waste hours of time sitting in trains doing nothing, so in addition to my case, I carried a portable typewriter with which I could transform each carriage into a mobile office, and I also carried a Uher tape recorder on my back. By now I was fully conversant with local radio, and often made recordings which I would send on for broadcasting.

My case was now a large one since I often had to be away for several days at a time. This also meant that I could no longer have just one suit and its accessories, and that, in turn, meant complications.

With one suit I have no choice to make. I simply get it out with the shirt and tie or whatever, and put it on. But with two sets of clothes I have to make sure that I get the right colour combinations. This is really Margaret's department.

On our occasional shopping expeditions for my clothes, I immediately know when she has decided something is right for me. If she looks at the garment and says 'That's quite nice', I know we won't be buying it. But if she says 'That's nice' - then that is the one we will buy!

Our next problem was how to arrange my clothes in the case so that I would know what went with what. This was achieved by buying a case with a large compartment in the lid. Into this Margaret puts the accessories which go with suit A, and the rest go in the body of the case together with suit B.

This system worked well for many years - except for one occasion when a very helpful hostess took my case up to my room, and came down to announce that she had unpacked it for me! I had to take pot luck with choices that week! When I got home, Margaret knew immediately that the system had failed. "What on earth's happened?" she said as she looked at my mis-matched accessories.

Now Margaret sees that I have colours which blend together, so that if I do inadvertently mix things, there is no real harm done.

Organisation in the clothes department may have solved one problem, but it created another. The case was now heavy, and with all the other things I had to carry around with me, I had no free hand to lead a guide dog. My faithful companion, Donna,

146

had died in 1971, but considering the problems of luggage, it was not really practical for me to apply for another dog. But I did not realise the danger I now was in.

I had an arrangement with Torch that when I was to go to Hurstpierpoint for a committee meeting, I would ring them from Hassocks station, and someone would drive out to pick me up.

On one memorable occasion, I arrived at Hassocks, but the train had been a very long one, and I knew that the platform here was very short. When I got off the train, I was a long way from the exit, and needed, therefore, to walk nearer to the point where my chauffeur would be able to spot me more easily. I began to walk towards the station area, but I was unaware what the weight of a loaded case in one hand did to the equilibrium.

Although I thought I was walking straight ahead, I was actually gradually veering towards the line. No-one noticed what was happening, and sure enough, with a dreadful shock, I fell about two metres down onto the line, together with all my luggage.

One of the railway employees was as shocked as I was. He rushed up and shouted at me;

"What the ******** are you doing down there? For goodness sake hurry up and get out of there - the London to Brighton express is due right now!"

Struggling to locate my typewriter and tape recorder, I was hauled up. Thankfully, my only injury was a damaged ankle, and I was grateful it had not been worse. The express did not arrive - there just happened to be a strike on at the time!

I was therefore overloaded, and made a decision that as soon as I could I would reorganise myself and apply for another guide dog. But for now, there was so much to do.

One opening had been through 'Word Records', who asked me to make a series of recordings. So the 'Instant Piano' series was made, and from the comments I received as I travelled around, they were appreciated by many people.

These were incredibly busy but wonderful times. There were

committee meetings, deputations, meetings with the Social Services, fellowship groups, gospel opportunities, and I continued to travel to Ireland a great deal.

In 1972 I was asked to take part in a programme for Radio 2 called 'The Gospel Road', which was hosted by Cliff Richard. Cliff was to interview me and I would talk about my life and work, and play the piano. Before the recording, however, we got together for a chat, and tried a song or two over together. They went very well and Cliff enthused:

"That was marvellous, man! We could really work together!"

As it happened, I had a terrible cold, and was in some difficulty with a sore throat. But Cliff had a handy remedy. He handed me a packet of throat sweets and said, "Here, try these," insisting that I kept the lot!

Later, when I indulged in a little 'name dropping' to a crowd of teenage girls, their first reaction was to ask me what I did with the packet. Mystified, I told them that when the sweets were gone I threw it away, of course. They were horrified! "Why didn't you keep it?" they said, nearly in tears!

I wasn't the only member of the Jackson family who was able to boast of having met Cliff Richard. My nephew, who was a vocalist for the pop group 'The Applejacks', also travelled in illustrious circles. His group became quite popular in the late 1960's, getting openings on television and with recordings. It was a hectic lifestyle, and although the pop scene was intoxicating for many young rising stars, it held all kinds of dangers both moral and physical for the unsuspecting youngsters. My nephew saw what was happening, and after a brief success, he became disillusioned with the pop scene, and left.

Life was very exciting. The many house parties were times of great blessing, some of which were held at Torch House in Hurstpierpoint, with blind people attending who had no idea what they were letting themselves in for!

Sarah came to a Torch houseparty fully equipped. Included in her luggage was a pair of dancing shoes which she expected to be using most evenings. On the first night, she came downstairs ready to begin a week of frenzied footwork, but was confused by the sound she heard. It was not the sound of a three piece combo beating out a quick-step, but the sound of loud voices singing hymns enthusiastically. Her heart sank.

"Good grief!" she complained to a friend in a quiet moment later. 'They're singing 'Once I was blind, but now I can see' - and they're all as blind as bats!" But it was not too long before she was joining in as enthusiastically as the rest.

Another girl, Frances, was fed up with all the talk about becoming a Christian.

"What's all the fuss about?" she asked. 'Surely being a Christian simply means that you're good and kind and try not to do anybody any harm."

"Would you like to know what the founder of Christianity said about it?" I asked her.

"Yes, I would," she replied. So I went on to explain what Jesus says about himself in the Bible. "He says 'I am the Way, and the Truth and the Life, no-one comes to the Father except through me'," I told her. We talked about this for a while, then I asked her to pray that God would show her how to be a Christian on *His* terms.

The next morning she said, "I am a Christian now, because I asked God to make me one on His terms!"

Dougal was a character. He was a partially-sighted permanent resident of the Torch House family, not just a visitor, and provided us all with some of our most enduring memories of the times there. He had had a sad life, having been abandoned on a doorstep as a baby, and taken to Barnardo's Homes. He had carried that rejection with him through life.

Now that he had been accepted into the Torch family, he lived in subconscious fear that he would be rejected again if he stepped out of line. So he was a Christian. He learned all the right words to say, and joined in all the singing enthusiastically, and gave every sign that he belonged.

Once when the folk were all out on a country walk together, Dougal fell behind.

"Keep up!" They all called, knowing that it would be safer if they all kept together.

"I'm all right!" yelled back Dougal, 'I'm not completely blind! I can manage." So the rest of the party stopped chivvying him, and went on.

Dougal arrived very late that evening. Everyone was becoming quite worried by the time he appeared.

"What happened?" They asked him. 'Where have you been?" It was quite evident how much sight Dougal actually had, by his explanation.

"I fell over a cow!" he said.

One evening when I was preaching, I told the houseparty clearly what it meant to be a Christian. Afterwards Dougal came to me and said venomously,

"I hate you."

"Oh dear," I replied. 'Why is that?"

"Because you have blown my cover," he responded accurately, but malevolently.

Dougal did not appear the next morning, and after breakfast we all went into the chapel for a short time together. Loudly, we sang, 'He sought me when I was wandering far away. He found me, he found me, O what a wonderful day!"

We had not realised that our singing travelled clearly up into Dougal's room and that during the song God had broken through to him. He cried, asking God to forgive him and make him a real member of His family. Later he came to me and put his arms around me.

"I hated you yesterday," he said, 'but I love you today!"

Blind people used to come from far and wide to share in these wonderful times. Here, as in meetings in other places, I was often asked to give my testimony and tell how I had come to know Jesus as my Saviour and Lord.

It was difficult to know where to begin at times like these. I could only skim over the surface of my memories, giving a rough idea as to how I developed my piano playing and how my ambitions changed from show business to evangelism. Then, as now, I would demonstrate the various styles of playing I went through, from my childhood attempts on the enforced classics of school days, and the contrasting pop idiom of my home in the holidays. Then I would tell how it all changed when I discovered that God loved me - and always had - and was waiting to show me a new way of living.

I would explain how there is no need to be afraid that we might not come up to God's expectations. God is never disillusioned with me because He never had any illusions in the first place! I pointed out that Jesus offers new life to anyone who will accept his offer of salvation.

What is even more difficult is explaining that I consider my blindness to be not so much a handicap as a gift from God which makes me, me. It is part of the essential me - something without which I could not be the kind of person I am today. I do not regret it. It would certainly be good to see my wife and my children, but I can say with confidence that because of what Jesus did, one day I will see them! Not only that, and even more wonderful - the first person I shall ever see will be Jesus himself!

My purpose of integrating the blind with the sighted could be very helpfully advanced by the use of local radio. I could attract their attention by the fact that I worked for Torch. Then, when I explained that I wanted to enlarge the horizons of the blind through integration, they usually did what they could to help.

Their motives were not entirely charitable - they knew that people were interested in hearing about the blind and that it would make for good audience ratings, but in any case, I was able to advance our cause. In those days I represented simply 'Torch Trust for the Blind, nowadays it would be a trust for the 'visually impaired'. Somehow it doesn't have the same emotive ring! At least we got the ears of the people - and that was good.

I used to use my Uher recorder which gave the very good

quality reproduction vital to the media, and would introduce Torch and say 'I'll be in your area on.........' Then I would send it to a local radio station. The following week I would probably be asked to do an interview with them for broadcasting. Before long, National Radio became interested, and I was able to take part in the 'In Touch' programme, and then my constant trips to Northern Ireland resulted in a lot of television work.

Even the prestigious 'Woman's Hour' of national radio became interested in the work of Torch. They got to hear that we had a ladies choir made up of staff and residents.

The choir usually sang in three-part harmony, and we got over the problem of written music and the learning of parts, by playing them onto cassettes so that each choir member could listen and learn individually. 'Woman's Hour' found this intriguing, and made a programme featuring the blind choir.

At last, in 1973, I got down to applying for another guide dog. This meant eventually being called for a weekend stay at the guide dog training centre at Leamington Spa. I did not need the full course because I had already trained with Donna.

On the Friday evening we were introduced to the staff and each other, and spent time settling in. On Saturday we went for a walk round the grounds to acclimatize to the surroundings, and then in the afternoon and evening there were instruction classes. We learned something about the psychology of dogs, how they are trained, and the necessary principles of handling.

We were assessed ourselves - our height, weight, the speed we walk, and the kind of work we do were all taken into account in choosing the right dog for each blind person. Dog and human were to be a unit.

Most of the time, the trainers decide what breed of dog each person should have, based on the personality of the dog and the assessment of the potential owner, but occasionally they take into account any specific requests.

This was so in my case, since my job took me constantly into people's homes, both as Torch representative, or as a tuner, and

I found many people to be wary of Alsatians. I thought it would be best to play safe and opt for a labrador if I could.

Sharing the course with me was a young woman I knew called Cathy. She had needed a guide dog for some time, but was very nervous of dogs, and could not bring herself to apply for one. It took a near disaster to bring her to the point where she could handle her fear.

She had been walking along one day with her white stick, when suddenly, like me on occasions, she had fallen down a badly protected manhole. This one, however, was no mere one or two metre drop. It was a long fall, down and down.

As she fell, Cathy told us afterwards that instead of her life flashing before her, she had recalled only one thing: a text from Romans chapter 8, verse 38; '.......I am convinced that neither...... height nor depth, nor anything else....... can separate us from the love of God.....'!

Miraculously she fell on her feet but she was terribly shaken, of course. The men working down the hole were nearly as surprised as she was:

"Where have you come from?" they asked, confused! When they had helped her to the surface again, Cathy resolved to apply for her guide dog.

She was still very nervous as she sat in her room at the centre waiting for a dog to be brought to see her, as was the custom. In her case, because she was so frightened, the staff decided to bring her a dog to get used to first. She would receive her own dog later, when she had got more used to the idea.

So there Cathy waited. She sat on her bed listening for the sound of footsteps and the gentle tapping of claws on the lino as they approached her room, and her heart thumped.

"Oh, Lord," she prayed, "please give me courage. You know how nervous I am".

Soon the expected sounds were heard, and a staff member knocked at the door. As they came in a voice said,

"Hello, Cathy, I've brought this dog to meet you - her name's

'Courage'"'! God could not have prepared Cathy more beautifully for this new stage of her life.

Later, when she received her own dog called Bonnie, they worked together confidently and soon became inseparable friends.

My new dog was 'Andy'. He was a beautiful and very sensitive golden labrador who proved to be far more nervous than Donna had been. He would shy away from a falling leaf! Yet he went on to serve me faithfully until he died.

Like all guide dogs, he was trained to act differently once he was fitted with his harness. When he was on duty, he was a reliable, intelligent helper. But take off the harness, and he became a lovable, unthinking pet. When given the chance to relax without the harness, he would forget all his training and not think twice about running straight into the road if there was something to attract his attention on the other side. But re-place the harness, and he became a model of attention, good sense and excellent behaviour!

Andy, however, was destined to achieve a certain notoriety.

One morning, Margaret received a phone call from the BBC. I was in Northern Ireland at the time, so Margaret got in touch with me urgently. It was nothing to do with my usual broadcasts, but was from the producers of the television programme 'Jim'll Fix It'. This is a 'make your dreams come true' kind of programme, where people of any age write in to say what they would most like to do. The extrovert personality of Jimmy Saville, sets to fixing for them to achieve their dream.

Apparently, some time before, while Andy was still in training, a boy and girl had written to ask if they could try out what it would be like to be led by a guide dog, and this had appealed to the producers. They had then contacted the Guide Dog Association, to ask if they would provide a dog for the programme.

Andy had been taken, and the 'dream' had been realised. The children were blindfolded, and Andy led them around the studio.

They were then presented with their 'Jim'll Fix It' badges, and Andy received a lot of welcome fuss for his part. But that did not turn out to be the end of the matter. The B.B.C. did not know it, but I had had a conversation with some lads one evening when I was at a meeting in Croydon. They came up to me and asked:

"Has your dog, Andy, ever been on 'Jim'll Fix It?'"

"That's right", I replied, 'did you watch the programme?"

"Yes, we did", they said, and then quickly added, 'Did Andy get a 'Jim'll Fix It' badge too?"

"Not as far as I know", I answered, 'it was only the children who wrote in who got the badges".

"That's not fair", they told me indignantly.

I promptly forgot the incident until we received the phone call from the BBC about a year after my conversation with the lads.

The B.B.C. continued: 'We have heard from some children who think it is very unfair that your dog did not receive a 'Jim'll Fix It' badge for his part in helping on an earlier programme. Would you like to bring the dog once more, so that we can put the matter right?"

So off I went with Andy to the television studios, and he was presented with his badge before the admiring audience. I tried to make him do his party trick by barking a 'thank you', but he was overcome by shyness and would not perform!

However, after his television appearances, I incorporated Andy into my children's talks by bringing out the large badge with its attached ribbon, and explaining that although 'Jim Fixed It' for Andy and the other children, God has 'fixed it' for us to be reunited with himself through the sacrifice of Jesus on Calvary!

And so Andy continued to travel with me everywhere, all over England and the British Isles, proving to be an invaluable companion and a very useful aid.

Chapter 16

THE END OF AN ERA

As the work of 'Torch' expanded with more and more people being reached world wide by the tape and Braille book ministry, and with fellowship groups opening up everywhere, the headquarters at Hurstpierpoint became too small. There were so many people to be accommodated - there were the everyday workers, the transcribers, the book and cassette readers and others. Its purpose began to change, too. Blind people began to want to visit the headquarters for one reason and another. There was 'Transcriber's Day', 'Prayer Partner's Day', and many other 'days', and then there were the houseparties - for the blind.Soon applications outstripped accommodation, and it was clear that new premises would have to be found if the work was to go on in this direction.

I was a little uneasy as I saw the increasing numbers of blind people gathering together day by day and in the houseparties. They were great times of fun and fellowship, of course, and everyone certainly enjoyed them,but it was the blind gathering together with the blind. My vision was that blind would gather with sighted and learn to integrate, but it seemed to me that we were in danger of moving away from this aim and going backwards into introversion instead.

However, a new location had to be found, and the search began. A house of the right size and price was, of course, difficult to find, but eventually one was discovered in Hallaton in Leicestershire. Hallaton Hall had been some kind of convent, and was in secluded grounds surrounded by a high wall and situated near the village.

I fully realised the problems involved in finding a house which would be able to cater for the needs of the work, but I could not suppress the uneasy feeling that was growing in my spirit. The house was indeed large enough, and I was sure it was in beautiful surroundings, but it was also remarkably secluded from life in general. Some would have taken that to be an advantage, I expect, but I could envisage dangers. It was in a quiet village miles from the nearest town of Market Harborough, and was entirely off the 'beaten track'. Then there was the wall. It all helped to add to the feeling of being cut off from society. I felt sure that the blind visitors would be one step further back into introversion instead of away from it.

The move was made in 1974, and already a new aspect of the work began to creep in. Rather strangely, a deliverance ministry developed. It began in a small way with one or two people being delivered from evil spirits and released into a new fellowship with God, but gradually more and more came forward for ministry.

As the work settled into Hallaton Hall, I was somewhat confused by the way things were going. It seemed to me that the deliverance ministry was beginning to take an unbalanced precedence. I supposed that this could be part of the work, but I was not entirely sure that God would lead so far in this direction that the original vision might possibly be overlooked.

However, it all began well. One of the first events was an Easter houseparty, at which Helen Roseveare, the famous missionary, was the speaker. This turned out to be wonderful, and a time of great blessing. The future looked rosy. 'Torch' was by now nationally known, and even the BBC was taking notice. Things were, indeed, looking up.

Yet still I had the uneasy feeling. The headquarters at Hurstpierpoint had been close to the town, and any visitors were well able to get around and integrate. At Hallaton Hall they were isolated and dependent. There was not even a local church to provide some outside contact, and inevitably, services took place within the Hall. Gradually, and surely, as I had predicted, the blind community - both resident and transient - became more introverted into itself.

In order to try to open up the possibilities again, I suggested that we form a church fellowship down in the village, to which the local people could come and join in with us. But sadly, although there were those on the staff who agreed with me, the Torch committee of about eight people, disagreed. I was over-ruled, and it was insisted upon that the fellowship remain in the Hall. Even the communion became the 'Torch Communion', and I felt that the backward march to introversion was complete.

There now began a further phenomenon, that of prophecy. This is a highly emotive subject within the modern Christian church, because in many cases it is impossible to test the credence of the prophecy - or, indeed, the prophet. Any Christian who is sincerely seeking for God's leading and blessing would certainly listen if someone purported to have a message from God. But the difficulty is in testing the prophecy for authenticity.

Unfortunately, many of the prophecies supposedly received at this time were against me and my aims for the work. I had, therefore, in all honesty, to look at what I was doing and saying, and pray earnestly that God would reveal to me any way in which I was stepping out of his will. It was a time of much heart searching and fervent prayer, but it only served to convince me further that my original vision was right, and that I could not go along with the present way of thinking.

I trust that throughout my Christian life I have always been prepared to give way to change if it should be necessary to avoid stagnation, and to continually be led by the Spirit of God in all I have tried to do. The situation in which I found myself, however, was unusual. I was outnumbered, and yet I could not get away from the feeling that I should not abandon my ideals, but remain with them. Sadly, this put me at a distinct disadvantage, and I was aware of a force of evil closing in around me.

In any good work for God, the devil will attempt to disrupt and destroy, and as the master of deception, spread dissent and confusion. In my situation, I experienced the full force of the devil's evil work, and in the face of allegations and suspicion brought about entirely through the devil's ability to deceive, I knew that the time had come for me to leave.

The end came destructively and crushingly. Where I had behaved foolishly, I requested forgiveness, and although God forgives, people don't. I found myself ostracised and condemned although I was never told what my real offences had been.

My work was at an end, and I fully believed my entire ministry was too.

When the devil pulls out all the stops to deceive, then no-one trusts anybody, and the truth is hidden in the maelstrom. Although, as is always the case in troubles such as this, the supposed offences are augmented way beyond actual events, I felt that I might never regain credibility, and that worse still, God's work was damaged beyond repair. Even Margaret did not know what to believe, and our marriage came under threat.

I was totally devastated. All my bookings were cancelled, and with a very heavy heart I wrote to my great friends in Northern Ireland to tell them that I would not be able to visit them any more because I could no longer represent the Torch Trust.

I felt completely isolated. I had no financial backing from anyone, and since my work for Torch was not conducive to joining a church fellowship, I could not even enlist the support of a church family. My ministry was finished, and I would never be able to work for God again.

Once more I had the additional problem of providing an income for my family. I would return to piano tuning, of course, but it would take time to build up a business. What would we do until we were self-sufficient? My despair new no bounds.

It was the people of Northern Ireland who came to my rescue.

Soon after receiving my despondant letter, they contacted me. They were anguished to hear what had happened, but instead of joining in the condemnation, they assured me that my ministry was far from over where they were concerned. They proved it by arranging to support me financially for a while until I had got myself together.

I can never express my gratitude to the folk of Northern Ireland for their help. They gave me more than practical assistance - they restored in me a new hope for the future, and the realisation that God had not finished with me, but was taking me on to something new.

I soon discovered that my ministry did not, after all, end with my association with Torch, but that I was still wanted as an evangelist in my own right. The bookings came back again, and people requested my help regardless of the broken partnership. God was picking me up and setting me on a different road.

The piano tuning went well, and I sought and obtained the education contract for South Leicestershire. It was not long before I was established.

By this time we had also become firm friends with some folk we met through the Filey conventions. They lived in Ammanford, South Wales, and we began going there for holidays. They belonged to a very small church fellowship which had no church building, but simply consisted of a few people meeting together in a little room of the Pensioner's Hall in Ammanford. When we were there I was asked to give a few Bible studies, and of course, I helped with the music. We thoroughly enjoyed our times of holiday in the completely new surroundings of the hills and valleys of Wales.

My independent work as an evangelist blossomed, with bookings in many places, and the work in Northern Ireland was unchanged. However, as my additional travelling for Torch was now finished, I looked forward to spending more time at home. Margaret and I rebuilt our relationship, and decided to cement it by increasing our family.

Bethany Clare was duly born on May 20th 1978 to the great delight of us all. Timothy and Christopher now had a little sister to dote on!

It was good to get back to the complete change of the tuning work, to meet people in a different context, and watch for opportunities to reach them with the love of God. Andy also came into his own as he led me around familiar territory, and together we settled into a more leisurely lifestyle.

I usually had no trouble in locating the homes of any new customers. I knew the area well, and if there should be a street I did not know, I could always ask someone. But sometimes there might be a problem in locating the exact house I needed. Often there might not be anyone to ask, and there is therefore no way I can tell which number is which. My only way out is to knock at a door and ask. I have learned, however, to choose my words carefully.

One day I approached what I hoped was the right house, and knocked at the door. A lady opened it and I unthinkingly asked her:

"Are you eighty-seven?" She slammed the door in my face, and I resolved to re-phrase my question in future!

Another lady in Solihull, having plied me with the usual coffee, (which I so often find nearly coming out of my ears after a day's tuning!) was telling me about her involvement with the local choir.

"We're doing 'Messiah'" she said, "my favourite piece is 'For Unto Us a Child is Born', but I can't understand what it means when it says 'Wonderful Counsellor', and about the 'government being on his shoulder'".

Having made sure that she really did want to know - my job being to tune her piano, not act as an evangelist - I was able to go on and explain that one day Jesus is going to come back and reign supreme with a new heaven and a new earth. Then I pointed out that for her, personally, it could mean that she could place the government of her life on Jesus' shoulders. He could live his life through hers if she would allow him, and she would then discover for herself how he could be the 'Wonderful Counsellor', the Mighty God and the Prince of Peace in her own life.

Some time later, she wrote to tell me that she had trusted the Lord there and then. This was the kind of experience that made my work exciting and fulfilling.

Another time, though, the tables were turned on me!

As soon as I walked into the house of my newest customer, I knew something was different. the lady did not lead me to the piano, but to an arm chair. She asked me if I would like a cup of tea, and although I didn't, experience taught me that refusal is often taken to be an insult, so I accepted compliantly.

The tea arrived, and so did a huge plate of cakes - all at 9.15 in the morning! I could do no more than accept the offer of a very large jam doughnut to add to my already substantial breakfast, and to listen to my hostess explaining that I was not to feel sorry for her since her husband died, because Jesus had promised to take care of her. Several fancy cakes and three cups of tea later, she was still telling me that Jesus would take care of me too, if I would let him!

Here was a lady doing her Christian duty and testifying to all she could about her faith in God. She was carrying out her personal evangelism obligation. She had forgotten only one thing, and that was to discover whether the object of her zeal was already a Christian! When she paused for breath , I grabbed the chance to say:

"Let's have a word of prayer......" I thanked God for her willingness to tell others about his saving power, and prayed that he would continue to take care of her. When I had finished, she gasped:

"Why didn't you tell me you were a Christian?"

"You didn't give me the chance!" I laughed.

Once when I was taking meetings in Devon, I called to see a man who had become blind in his fifties. It is always more difficult to come to terms with such a radical change later in life, and I asked him if he would be interested in learning Braille, and getting some books to read.

"There is also a talking book service," I offered. "Would you be interested in taking advantage of it?"

"What would I need a talking book for?" he retorted, 'I married one, didn't I?"

During 1981, Andy and I shared another very special occasion. It was the Jubilee of the Guide Dog Association, and it took place in Westminster Abbey. I was very honoured to be one of those chosen to have tea in the Royal Mews with Princess Alexandra, the Patroness of the organisation. I sometimes liked to take one of the family with me to special functions, so that I could be sure of any necessary help, and this time I took thirteen-year-old Tim.

Six hundred guide dogs and owners assembled in the Abbey, and all the dogs settled down for the long wait as the service went on.

It was inspiring and uplifting, and we eagerly waited for the address from the specially invited guest, Lord Tonypandy, who was at the time, George Thomas, Speaker of the House of Commons. He looked down at all the guide dogs lying obediently and patiently at their owner's feet, and in his inimitable fashion said :

"I wish....... I wish........ I could get that kind of order in my place of work!"

At the end of the service when the benediction had been announced, with one accord the entire company of dogs rose to their feet......... and SHOOK! It sounded like a huge flock of birds taking off!

But we still had the reception with Princess Alexandra to follow, and Tim, Andy and I went off proudly to be presented. The Princess was quite charming - a delightful lady, and she talked very kindly to Tim who was absolutely thrilled.

Her bodyguards were not quite so thrilled however, when Andy seemed particularly interested in the princess, and got very close to her. An equerry told me quietly what was happening, and I apologised.

"I'm very sorry," I said, "I'm afraid he's very, very fussy about the company he keeps!" The princess laughed, and the interview was ended.

Chapter 17

A NEW CHAPTER

In 1980, we received a telephone call which was to lead to a new beginning for us all. The call was from our friends in South Wales, and they told us that their little fellowship was growing, and that they now met in the St. John's Ambulance hall in Ammanford. But they had something else in mind.

"We would like you to come and head up the work for us,"they said, 'would you think about it, and pray, and consider moving here to help with the work?"

We did think and pray, and we did not take very long to come to the conclusion that this was probably God's way of giving us all a new start after the sadness of the break with Torch.

We agreed to move, but there would be the initial problem of selling our house in Market Harborough before being able to re-buy in Ammanford. We put it up for sale, confident that in view of the fact that we were moving with the Lord's approval, he would see to it that the house sold reasonably quickly.

People came to view, but nobody got as far as actually buying it. There were those who liked it, but they had to sell their own house, so there was the problem of the 'chain'. We began to wonder if we had got the Lord's will right or not.

Nearly two years went by, and we began to despair. What could have gone wrong? We prayed and wondered, and decided that we would wait until the end of July. Then if the house had not sold, that would be final. We would take it off the market, and assume that we had got the whole thing wrong and that God wanted us to remain in Market Harborough.

Half way through July, two sisters came to view the house with their father. They were local girls and were looking for a place to share together. Margaret and I were not hopeful. It seemed very unlikely that two single sisters would want a four bedroomed house.

They walked around, and the girls' father stood with me as the others went through on to the patio.

"They'll buy it, you know," he told me confidently, '.....and it'll be a cash sale - their company will be buying it for them - something to do with tax.......," he went on conspiratorially.

We had the money within a week. Excitedly, we rang the estate agent in South Wales to tell him that we could now go ahead with the bungalow we had seen in Ammanford.

"Oh," he said guardedly, "there is already someone else interested in that one now, I'm afraid it will go to the one who can come up with the cash first."

We put the wheels in motion immediately, and we beat the other buyer by one day! The beautiful bungalow in Wales was ours!

There was so much to look forward to - new surroundings, new people, and a new church. It was all very exciting. Of course, I would need to set up a whole new piano tuning business again, but I had not had a great deal of problems in that respect before, and surely in the 'Land of Song' there ought to be plenty of pianos to keep in order!

It was good to be with all our Welsh friends again, and this time we would not be returning to England after a couple of weeks. I began my work with the church, and also set to building up the piano tuning business which did, indeed, take off encouragingly, and we settled into our new surroundings.

My colleagues of the church fellowship were well versed with my independent work as an evangelist, and they knew that when I came to join them, I would still have many bookings to honour elsewhere. They also, very graciously, mentioned that they did not want to confine God's work by restricting my ministry entirely to themselves. So it was agreed that I would spend basically one weekend every month away, ministering elsewhere.

However, there would be times when I would have to be away longer, such as when I had to go to Northern Ireland, but I assured them that I would try to ensure that my trips away did not interfere too much with the work of the fellowship.

I soon settled down to my usual routine, and with it, my continued age-old problem - that of earning enough money to fund the trips I make. My travels cost a great deal in transport expenses alone, but there is also the time lost when I am not available to tune pianos, plus the time spent in study and preparation for each meeting. Even a weekend away reasonably near home will mean that I lose the income of Saturday's tuning, but a longer journey will mean travelling on the Friday or maybe even earlier, with a return on Monday or Tuesday after the Sunday night meetings. Very quickly I find that I have lost nearly a week's salary in order to undertake two days of meetings.

The problem is a difficult one since many churches do not have the resources to fund the cost of such an undertaking, but more often, the full implications of inviting a speaker are not completely realised. I have spoken to many fellow ministers and colleagues over the years who have struggled with the same problem. They are anxious to visit other fellowships when asked, but the small honorarium usually offered is simply not enough to enable them to accept the invitation. So often, like them, I find that the gift does not even cover my train fare.

God has promised to supply all our needs, and he undoubtedly does, but he has also said that 'the worker is worth his keep' (Matthew 10; verse 10), so there is an obligation upon those who hire the worker to pay him. But God's promise of provision also applies to the churches who do the hiring, so there really should be no problem!

If the churches pray and ask God for direction and provision for the support of a hired worker, then He will either supply the financial need, or indicate that they should not hire in the first place.

But I still continue to work to keep not only my family and everyday obligations, but to fund my evangelistic work as well.

By now, I had a very good friend in Ireland who, in effect, was acting as my 'agent'. I had stayed with Harold and Meta Patterson many times during my trips there, and he had slipped into a role of 'arranger' between myself and the churches who wanted me to visit them. He would completely organise any tour, relieving me of the problem of fixing up accommodation, travel and other details.

But it was not only the churches that Harold arranged for me to visit. I had learned to my cost that wherever God has a successful work, the devil will take trouble to spoil it. Conversely, wherever the devil has a particular foothold, God will prove that he is in ultimate control by overcoming the evil with good. No where is this more apparent than in the prisons of Northern Ireland where terrorists have been reached and changed completely by the Spirit of God.

Much media time and effort is given over to the publicity of the atrocities, but very little is reported about the many transformations experienced by prisoners who have come to realise that God is not the God of the Catholic or the Protestant, but of the sinner. Throughout my years of visiting Northern Ireland, I have had the privilege of being invited into the prisons, along with others, and bringing the love of God and the gospel of a new life in Christ to those who would listen. Many have listened, and responded.

One of my weekend trips was to take part in a houseparty which included twelve ex-terrorists whose lives had been changed by the Lord Jesus Christ. It was a tremendous time, with men who had once been filled with hate, but who were now filled with love, and overflowing with praise.

Then on another visit, I was invited to have tea with prisoners who received me with affection and presented me with a special gift. They gave me a 'Gideon' Bible which had a beautiful leather case made by the prisoners themselves. Inside the Bible was an inscription. It said: 'God bless you, from the members of the UDA Long Kesh'. Yes, there was much blessing within the unlikely walls of the prisons, and I always look forward to each new visit with eager anticipation.

Throughout many years of ministry I have led many meetings and spoken to many people about the love of God and how Jesus paid the penalty for sin through his life and death, but it is wonderful now to sometimes meet those who responded to the message I brought so long ago.

A lady in her late twenties came to me in Belfast, one day. She said:

"I am a Christian, but part of the process which brought me to God happened when I was a fifth former and you came to talk to us at school. That was thirteen years ago, and I still remember what you said that day."

The very first coffee bar crusade which took place in Northern Ireland was in 1971. I was part of a team from a church which set up a place where young people could be encouraged to come and have a cup of coffee and listen to the Gospel. I would play the piano, and then give a talk which would be a challenge to follow the Lord Jesus Christ. They were good times, but it was doubly wonderful when I returned to the same church in 1988 and the minister introduced me to a young man.

"This is Jack," he said, "he met you a few years ago."

"Yes," said Jack, "it was back in the coffee bar. I gave my heart to the Lord that night, after hearing your testimony." I was thrilled to have played a part in Jack's coming to salvation.

"You did a good job that night," continued the minister with his hand on Jack's shoulder. "This fellow is now my right-hand man - the chief of my elders here at the church."

In 1989 my travels went even further afield. Harold and Meta Patterson had a son, Trevor, who for two years took a teaching post in a Christian school in Nairobi, Kenya. He had a lot of contacts with churches around the area where he worked, and Harold and Meta thought it would be a good thing if I could go out and visit, dividing the time between ministry and a holiday.

It was duly all arranged, and I was able to take Margaret and

Bethany with me, too.

On the outward flight, Bethany went onto the flightdeck, and looked down at the map spread below her.

"What's that village down there?" she asked the crew.

"That 'village' is Cairo," they laughed.

Later she was telling someone about the experience, and said, "I saw a little village called Cairo way below us..."

"What?" said her companion. 'That's the biggest city in Africa!"

At one point we travelled out into the bush to visit the missionaries, Ronnie and Maggie Briggs, from Northern Ireland. They lived very primitively amongst the Masai people, miles from anywhere. On our way there, we were stopped by fearsome looking Masai warriors complete with spears, and all our pre-conceived ideas about cannabilistic tribesmen flashed into our minds. For a moment or two we were terrified as the men asked us where we were going.

"We are on our way to visit Ronnie and Maggie Briggs," we explained nervously.

The mens faces lit up into a broad, white-toothed grin.

'Ah! Bwana Briggs!" They shouted, and waved us on happily.

Another of my most vivid memories of the visit was being taken to the place where elephants go to drink. We had a picnic near the spot, and I was led down to the water's edge, where I put my feet into the footprints made by the elephants. It was a wonderful experience!

Beth was not so happy with an experience she had with the Masai women. She was dressed sensibly in trousers, to get around more comfortably amongst the wildness of the bush, and she also wore a cap to keep the sun off her head. Another mistake, was probably that she had the Briggs' youngest daughter, Naomi, on her back.

Suddenly they came across a group of Masai women who, on seeing what they thought was a girl dressed in boy's clothes, hurled abuse at her! Beth tried to cover her hair up with the cap to make herself look more like a boy, but it was a hopeless task, for the fact that she had a child on her back declared her to be a girl, absolutely and finally in the minds of the Masai women. Beth could do no more than run back home as fast as possible!

It was a wonderful time, however, and we travelled around seeing the sights and being spoiled dreadfully! We spent three weeks enjoying wonderful times of fellowship, holiday and ministering, and it certainly whetted my appetite for Africa! Perhaps we will be able to return some day.

Since we have lived in South Wales, my work has become increasingly noticed by Radio Wales. Most recently, in 1992, they asked me if they could make a documentary programme about me.

To begin with they attended a meeting I led in Newbridge, Gwent, and recorded the entire evening. Then they interviewed me at length, using both the meeting and the interview to put together a twenty-five minute documentary.

The programme included some of the interview, plus testimony and music. I explained that only God can make a disability into His ability, and I demonstrated the different kinds of playing necessary in the work - improvisation, congregational accompaniment and solo work, and I talked a bit about my travelling in years gone past, and my hopes for the future.

My next milestone is likely to involve America, where I have been asked to make a tour. This is somewhere I have always wanted to visit, and I look forward to it with great interest.

As Tim and Chris grew up, it was inevitable that they would become interested in piano tuning work, and after one or two fleeting attempts to climb out of the mould, they gave in and both finished up at the college of piano technology. They are now extremely good workmen, who are well able to transform a sadly neglected piano relic into an instrument of beauty. We now form a good team - Chris and I (on the whole) cope with the tuning, while Tim has a workshop and saleroom where he performs miracles of transformation on old instruments, and also sells new ones.

Margaret does her bit by dealing with the paper work, although she has taken on some part-time nursing so that she 'keeps her hand in'. Beth, however, is as yet, still working her way through her GCSE examinations. We await with interest to see where she will fit in to the scheme of things!

I now look forward to a retirement sometime in the future which will not confine me to a chair by the fireside, (or even the radiator!) but will allow me to travel around and preach God's word in greater freedom.

Although Margaret prefers to remain at home rather than continually live out of suitcases, it would be nice to take our time and enjoy some of my travels together. Perhaps this will be more possible in the years to come.

God has been very good to us throughout our lives together. We have had a great deal of joy, and some sadness, but we have always been aware of the presence of God in everything.

Even blindness has been, for me, an example of God's provision. It has made me the kind of person he wanted me to be. If I was sighted, I would be a completely different character and would probably have completely different gifts.

I thank him for the way he has moulded my life and directed me into glorifying his name through the gifts he gave me. I do not hanker for sight, but one day I will be like him - perfect in everything. On that day, I will open my eyes and see his face. then I will look for Margaret, Tim, Chris and Beth. One day I *will* see them!

'I will see you again and you will rejoice, and no-one will take away your joy.'
(John 16: 22)